The Everything Book
for Child Care & Preschool

Reproducible Checklists, Documentation & Assessment Forms,
Newsletters, Planners, Schedules & Decorative Borders
That Meet Every Child Care Need

by
Melissa Fisch & Kelly Gunzenhauser

illustrated by

Ron Kauffman & Vanessa Countryman

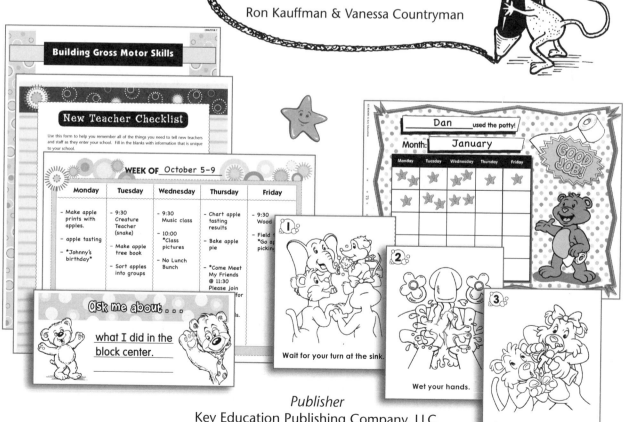

Publisher
Key Education Publishing Company, LLC
Minneapolis, MN 55438
www.keyeducationpublishing.com

CONGRATULATIONS ON YOUR PURCHASE OF A KEY EDUCATION PRODUCT!

The editors at Key Education are former teachers who bring experience, enthusiasm, and quality to each and every product. Thousands of teachers have looked to the staff at Key Education for new and innovative resources to make their work more enjoyable and rewarding. We are committed to developing educational materials that will assist teachers in building a strong and developmentally appropriate curriculum for young children.

PLAN FOR GREAT TEACHING EXPERIENCES WHEN YOU USE EDUCATIONAL MATERIALS FROM KEY EDUCATION PUBLISHING COMPANY, LLC

About the Authors

Melissa Fisch has a degree in early childhood education and has been a preschool teacher for 18 years. She has also taught music and movement to preschoolers for six years. Melissa has raised two boys—one attends middle school and the other attends high school. She spends most of her spare time driving them to baseball, basketball, and volleyball practice.

Kelly Gunzenhauser has a master's degree in English and taught writing at the college level. She has worked in educational publishing for 11 years and is the author of eight books for teachers and children. Kelly has two sons in preschool and spends her time playing and learning with them and volunteering at their school.

Acknowledgments

We would like to thank the following people: Fran Thull for her excellent advice about holiday celebrations, and April Cochrane and Heather Barrier for their cute ideas for interviewing children about their parents. M. F. & K. G.

Key Education welcomes manuscripts and product ideas from teachers. For a copy of our submission guidelines, please visit our Web site or send a self-addressed, stamped envelope to:

Key Education Publishing Company, LLC
Acquisitions Department
7309 West 112th Street
Minneapolis, Minnesota 55438

Credits

Authors: Melissa Fisch & Kelly Gunzenhauser
Publisher: Sherrill B. Flora
Illustrators: Ron Kauffman & Vanessa Countryman
Editors: Debra Olson Pressnall & Karen Seberg
Cover Design & Production: Annette Hollister-Papp
Page Layout: Debra Olson Pressnall
Cover Photographs: © ShutterStock

Copyright Notice

Standard Book Number: 978-1-602680-84-5
The Everything Book for Child Care & Preschool
Copyright © 2010 by Key Education Publishing Company, LLC
Minneapolis, Minnesota 55438

TABLE OF CONTENTS

INTRODUCTION

Child-care providers and preschool teachers and directors are constantly using forms. Need parents to donate supplies? Send a supply request form. Need to hire a new teacher? Pass out job applications to candidates. Teaching a student who bites? Send home a note about how to deal with biting. Need to schedule conferences? Use a sign-up sheet. Forms are necessary to keep communication going at a child-care or preschool facility. Since there are few resources that cover all of the bases, the forms that you currently use may be scattered all over and may not have a professional look. Perhaps, some are so old that you don't even remember where you got them. And, since you need new forms every now and then—for example, when a child with a peanut allergy joins a class—you must spend valuable time creating and recreating them.

The Everything Book for Child Care & Preschool is designed to cut down on your workload, make your forms more consistent, and polish your facility's or school's image. Included in this resource are student documentation and assessment forms, planning sheets, schedules, templates for invitations, parent communication notes, newsletters about common subjects, and tons of other helpful resources and great ideas that will make your communication with teachers, parents, and children as smooth and simple as possible all year long. Certain forms also have space to drop in your school's logo, and we have included decorative borders to help you make eye-catching messages.

So, get inspired by this resource book and put your best foot forward during the next preschool year!

CALENDAR PAGES

These generic calendar pages will help with scheduling, planning, and organizing information to share. To give them a customized look, make a reduced copy of the selected form (if needed), attach your school logo in the corner, and then make a second photocopy. The **Daily Routine** form may also be trimmed down and copied on one of the full-page decorative border sheets (pages 108–123) to make an attractive chart for parents to view.

Use the **Monthly Calendar** (page 7) to keep track of days off, school events, staff or student birthdays, staff meetings, professional training meetings, and holiday parties. Directors should consider filling out a calendar page for each month after the school schedule is finalized, making a copy for each teacher, and distributing them with a beginning-of-the-year packet. Teachers can hand out this calendar to parents in lieu of, or in addition to, a newsletter.

Use the **Weekly Planner** (page 8) to block out times for meetings, special visitors, or special classes and to add reminders for extra needs like supplies for upcoming projects. Larger space is provided so that you can make detailed notes.

The **Daily Routine** (page 9) is the map of your day. You can use this form in two ways. One way is to block out how you spend each day. When do you want to have circle time? When do students eat snacks? When is your outside time? You can also use this form as a record of events. For example, if Hunter learns to write his name or masters skipping for the first time, you can jot it on the day's daily record as a reminder to put that information in his file for later.

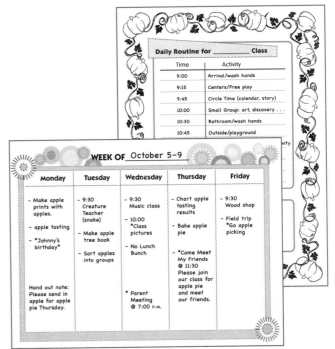

 ● **GOOD IDEA!** ● At the beginning of the year when you plan your daily schedule, make sure you include washing hands each time students walk into the classroom or get ready to eat. This helps prevent spreading illnesses. Plus, if you enforce it as a part of the daily schedule, it will become routine for children and it will not appear as if you made them wash up just when the accreditation inspectors came!

 ● **GOOD IDEA!** ● Post your daily schedule outside the classroom for times when students are late. If you are not in the classroom, then the parent will know where to find the class. If your daily schedule needs adjusting for any reason (such as for a special class), be sure to change the copy outside your door. You can do this simply with a sticky note.

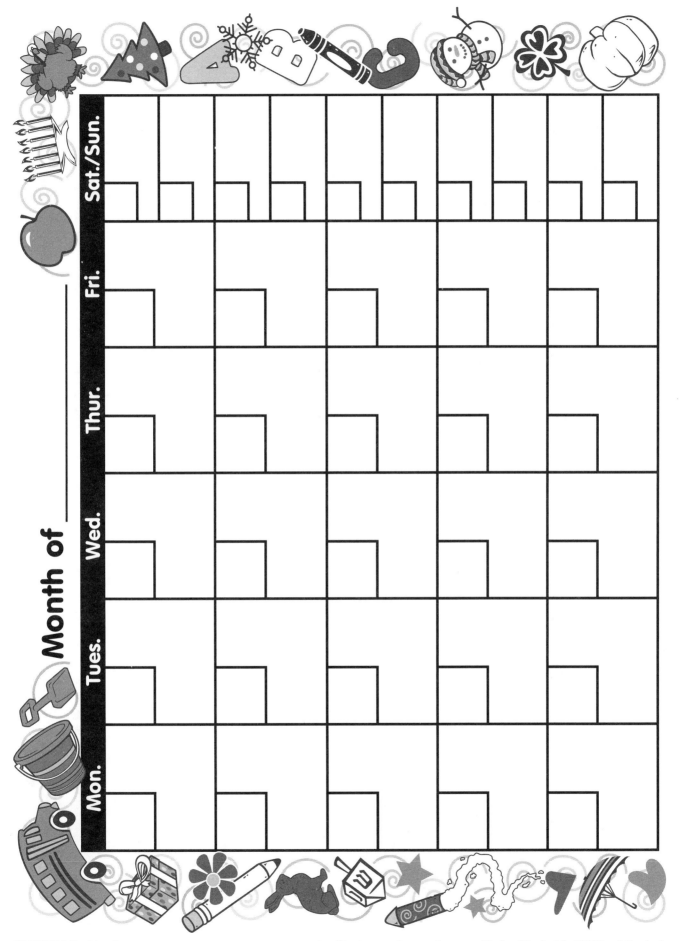

Month of _____

Mon.	Tues.	Wed.	Thur.	Fri.	Sat./Sun.

WEEK OF

Monday	Tuesday	Wednesday	Thursday	Friday

See page 6 for additional tips.
*Use one of the borders in Chapter 6
to decorate the sheet.*

Daily Routine for _____ Class

Time	Activity

Special Days

FORMS FOR THE DIRECTOR

Directors must have many forms that pertain to teachers, parents (as they have contact with the director), and the school or facility. These will help keep staff information organized, giving directors more time to interact with teachers, parents, and children.

This section starts off with the forms needed for hiring a new teacher, including a **Staff Employment Application** (pages 12 and 13), **Applicant Interview Checklist** (page 14), and **Reference Check Questions** (page 15). The **Staff Medical Form** (page 16) and **Staff Emergency Information Card** (page 17) will help document medical conditions of new and existing staff members. The **New Teacher Checklist** (page 18) is a reminder of everything a new teacher needs to know, including "odd" information to help her learn the ropes. (An example might include telling a new teacher that the back door sticks open.)

Ongoing staff management forms include a **Staff Evaluation Form** (pages 19 and 20), a form on which directors can keep a **Record of Staff Development Hours** (page 21), and a **Teacher and Class Assignment Chart** (page 22) that will help directors organize who works with whom, in what classroom, and with what age group of students. As a way to gather feedback from staff members, the **Beginning-of-the-Year Staff Questionnaire** and **End-of-the-Year Staff Questionnaire** (pages 23 and 24) can be used to get to know the teachers better. These forms will also offer educators opportunities to communicate their thoughts, observations, and preferences.

It takes plenty of planning to keep things running smoothly at a preschool or day-care facility. The **Staff Meeting Planner** (page 25) will help directors structure staff meetings thoughtfully. *A special tip:* At the beginning of the meeting, determine as a group how much time will be spent on each topic and then record that information on the sheet. By keeping all of the staff members on task during the meeting, it is then likely that all relevant topics will be discussed.

> ● **GOOD IDEA!** ●
>
> There are endless possible topics for staff meetings, such as outdoor play, curriculum discussions, CPR certification, a visit from an allergist, guidelines for using resources, safety plans, and general staff concerns and discussions.

Teachers should use the **Purchase Request** form (page 26) when they need funds to make a classroom purchase. Teachers can fill out copies of the request form and turn them into the director for approval. In some situations, teachers may need to fill in pertinent information on copies of the **Reimbursement Form** (page 26) and submit them with their corresponding receipts for reimbursement. (This system can be modified according to how money is distributed at your preschool or day-care facility.)

A director can use the **Director's Daily Schedule Planner** (page 28) both as a worksheet to plan a specific day or to post outside the office door to remind parents and teachers of standing meetings and commitments. (See a sample schedule on page 27.) To keep the channels of communication open, consider utilizing the **Director Evaluation Form** (pages 29 and 30) to gather feedback from teachers and paraprofessionals on a director's performance.

The handy **Parent Tour Checklist** (page 31) is an effective tool for directors to use as a reminder to highlight all important features about the preschool or child-care facility while showing prospective parents around.

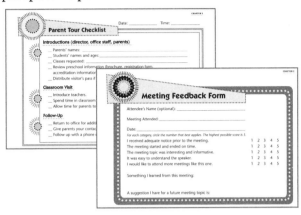

The last group of forms elicits opinions and help from parents. The **Parent Survey** (page 32) can be used as is or as a template for any type of survey to give parents in order to get their feedback. The **Meeting Feedback Form** (page 33) will solicit responses about recent teacher and parent meetings. The **Fund-Raiser & Event Summary** sheet (page 34) will help parent leaders evaluate their fund-raising events. During those times when volunteers are being recruited for fund-raisers or school and classroom events, posting a copy of the **Volunteers Needed!** sign-up sheet (page 35) will speed up the process. The **Essential Topics for Staff/Parent Orientation** (page 36) will serve as a reminder to cover all of the bases for a parent meeting at the beginning of the year. Incorporating some **Team-Building Activities for Teachers, Parents & Children** (page 37) can add to the fun.

Although these forms are designed for directors, some of them, such as the Record of Staff Development Hours; the Parent Tour Checklist; the Volunteers Needed! sign-up sheet; and the Team-Building Activities for Teachers, Parents & Children, can be very helpful for teachers, too.

STAFF EMPLOYMENT APPLICATION

Position Desired: _____   Circle one: Full-time   Part-time   Substitute

PERSONAL INFORMATION

Your Name: _____

Present Address: _____

Home Phone: _____   Cell Phone: _____

How long at above address? _____   Previous Address: _____

_____

E-mail Address: _____

EDUCATION

Type of School	Name	Location	Diploma or Degree	Date
High School				
Technical College				
College/University Undergraduate				
Graduate School				

WORK EXPERIENCE

List most recent employment first.

Employer Name and Address	Type of Work/Duties	Dates Employed

Employer Name and Address	Type of Work/Duties	Dates Employed

May we contact your current employer? _____   When can you begin work? _____

APPLICANT REFERENCES

Please list at least three references of people who have first-hand personal and professional knowledge of you.

Name:_____

Address: _____

Phone Number: _____

E-mail Address: _____

Relationship to Applicant: _____

Name:_____

Address: _____

Phone Number: _____

E-mail Address: _____

Relationship to Applicant: _____

Name:_____

Address: _____

Phone Number: _____

E-mail Address: _____

Relationship to Applicant: _____

Name:_____

Address: _____

Phone Number: _____

E-mail Address: _____

Relationship to Applicant: _____

ADDITIONAL INFORMATION

Please answer these questions on another sheet of paper.

Why do you want to work with young children? Why did you choose to apply for a job at our facility? How can you make our program stronger? What is the hardest part about being a preschool educator? List relevant qualifications, volunteer activities, or organizations to which you belong.

I have completed this application truthfully and to the best of my ability. I understand that if any information I provided is found to be false, I will be ineligible for employment.

Signature: _____   Date: _____

APPLICANT INTERVIEW CHECKLIST

Applicant's Name: _____   Interview Date: _____

Describe your previous job experiences.

What did you like and dislike most about previous jobs?

List three strengths you will bring to our program.

List three weaknesses you would like to improve.

Describe your attendance, punctuality, and reliability. Do you arrive at work on time? Do you have frequent absences? Please explain any issues you may have in this area.

Are you a team player? How well do you work with others?

How do you handle conflict with a co-worker? A parent? Between children?

Other questions or comments:

REFERENCE CHECK QUESTIONS

Applicant's Name: _____ Interview Date: _____

Name of Person Giving Reference: _____

Address: _____

Phone Number: _____ E-mail Address: _____

What is your relationship to the applicant? How long have you known the applicant?
Please describe the applicant's punctuality and reliability.
Please describe how the applicant got along with co-workers and supervisors. Is the applicant a team player?
The applicant is being considered for the position of _____. Do you think the applicant is a good fit? Why or why not?
What are the applicant's greatest strengths?
Do you have any other comments about the applicant?

IIIIIIIIIIIIIIIII STAFF MEDICAL FORM IIIIIIIIIIIIIIIII

Staff Member/Applicant's Name: _____

Address: _____

Home Phone Number: _____

To Be Completed by the Staff Member's Physician

This staff member/applicant will be expected to lift small children. Some additional lifting may be required. Additionally, this staff member/applicant will be responsible for the care of small children. Please answer the questions below regarding the health and fitness of the staff member/applicant.

Does this staff member/applicant have any physical or mental condition that will limit or detract from her/his ability to work with children? If yes, please explain.
Is this staff member/applicant receiving any medical treatment/medication that will limit or detract from her/his ability to work with children? If yes, please explain.
In your professional opinion, is this person physically, mentally, and emotionally qualified to care for children? If not, please explain.

Physician's Signature: _____ Date: _____

Office Location/Address: _____

STAFF EMERGENCY INFORMATION CARD

Name:_____

Address (Number & Street): _____

City: _____ State: _____ Zip Code: _____

Home Phone: _____ Cell Phone: _____

E-mail Address: _____

EMERGENCY CONTACTS

1. Name: _____ Relationship: _____

   Home Number: _____ Cell Number:_____

2. Name: _____ Relationship: _____

   Home Number: _____ Cell Number:_____

Hospital Preference: _____

Primary Physician: _____ Phone:_____

Allergies and Other Medical Concerns:

STAFF EMERGENCY INFORMATION CARD

Name:_____

Address (Number & Street): _____

City: _____ State: _____ Zip Code: _____

Home Phone: _____ Cell Phone: _____

E-mail Address: _____

EMERGENCY CONTACTS

1. Name: _____ Relationship: _____

   Home Number: _____ Cell Number:_____

2. Name: _____ Relationship: _____

   Home Number: _____ Cell Number:_____

Hospital Preference: _____

Primary Physician: _____ Phone:_____

Allergies and Other Medical Concerns:

New Teacher Checklist

Use this form to help you remember all of the things you need to tell new teachers and staff as they enter your school. Fill in the blanks with information that is unique to your school.

- ☐ Entry and exit procedures (sign in and sign out, security code if applicable)
- ☐ Office staff and custodial staff introductions
- ☐ Teacher introductions
- ☐ Office supply locations (paper, copier, fax machine, phone system, office computer, etc.)
- ☐ Restrooms for staff
- ☐ Restrooms for children
- ☐ Cleaning supplies and special cleaning procedures
- ☐ Snack and meal supplies
- ☐ Designated eating areas for students
- ☐ Designated eating areas for staff
- ☐ Meal procedures
- ☐ Teacher resource rooms (laminator, paper cutter, die cutter, classroom supplies)
- ☐ Art supply areas
- ☐ Library
- ☐ Other indoor play areas (gym, stage, music room, etc.)
- ☐ Playground

- ☐ Playground equipment storage
- ☐ Procedure for taking class outside
- ☐ Unloading bus procedures
- ☐ Loading bus procedures
- ☐ Fire drill
- ☐ Tornado drill
- ☐ Other emergency plans of action (intruder, CPR, injury, etc.)
- ☐ Inclement weather policy
- ☐ School closing policy
- ☐ School schedule
- ☐ Classroom
- ☐ Daily schedule (playground time, snack time, lunch time, special classes, etc.)
- ☐ Class roster
- ☐ Illness plans (allergic reaction, vomiting, diarrhea, fever, etc.)
- ☐ Reimbursement form
- ☐ Class parent procedures and forms
- ☐ _____
- ☐ _____
- ☐ _____

STAFF EVALUATION FORM

STAFF MEMBER: _____ DATE:_____

SUPERVISOR: _____

For each category, circle the number that best applies. The highest possible score is 5.

CLASSROOM MANAGEMENT

Classroom is inviting.	1 2 3 4 5
Classroom materials are developmentally appropriate, labeled, and organized.	1 2 3 4 5
Classroom is reasonably clean and safe for all students.	1 2 3 4 5
Staff member is well prepared each day.	1 2 3 4 5
Daily schedule is flexible to accommodate various classroom situations.	1 2 3 4 5
Learning goals are set for each student and based on daily observations.	1 2 3 4 5
Lesson plans reflect students' needs and are developmentally appropriate.	1 2 3 4 5
Transition time activities and methods are appropriate and effective.	1 2 3 4 5

INTERACTIONS WITH STUDENTS

Greets students by first name.	1 2 3 4 5
Responds to students calmly, promptly, and at their eye level.	1 2 3 4 5
Is respectful and kind to each student.	1 2 3 4 5
Encourages each student's individual talents.	1 2 3 4 5
Celebrates students' accomplishments in the area of self-help skills.	1 2 3 4 5
Fosters friendships between students.	1 2 3 4 5
Uses positive reinforcement to manage behaviors.	1 2 3 4 5

INTERACTIONS WITH PARENTS

Quickly learns to identify parents of each student.	1 2 3 4 5
Responds to parents' concerns promptly and professionally.	1 2 3 4 5
Communicates effectively with parents on a daily, weekly, and monthly basis.	1 2 3 4 5
Offers conference times twice a year or as needed.	1 2 3 4 5
Maintains confidentiality with parents and staff members.	1 2 3 4 5

WORK HABITS

Works as a team member with staff.	1 2 3 4 5
Contributes to a positive working environment.	1 2 3 4 5
Willingly mentors new staff members	1 2 3 4 5
Shows generosity with classroom materials and teaching information.	1 2 3 4 5
Is flexible and willing to help out in other areas as needed.	1 2 3 4 5
Arrives at work on time.	1 2 3 4 5
Follows absence and vacation policies.	1 2 3 4 5

STAFF MEMBER DEVELOPMENT

Has completed CPR and first-aid training.	1 2 3 4 5
Has accumulated required staff development hours.	1 2 3 4 5
Shares new ideas acquired from development with other staff members.	1 2 3 4 5
Incorporates newly learned information into classroom.	1 2 3 4 5

EVALUATOR'S COMMENTS

STAFF MEMBER'S COMMENTS

GOALS ACCOMPLISHED (See previous evaluation from _____.)
                                                                  Date

NEW GOALS SET (See previous evaluation from _____.)
                                                         Date

EVALUATOR'S SIGNATURE: _____ DATE:_____

STAFF MEMBER'S SIGNATURE: _____ DATE:_____

Record of Staff Development Hours

Name of Training	Given by & Date	Location	Credit Hours

All training certificates are attached to show verification of credit hours. _____ _____
                                                                                Yes   No

Staff Member's Signature: _____ Date: _____

Director's Signature: _____ Date: _____

Teacher and Class Assignment Chart

	Room Number	Teacher 1	Teacher 2	Teacher 3	Age Group
M MONDAY					
T TUESDAY					
W WEDNESDAY					
TH THURSDAY					
F FRIDAY					

Beginning-of-the-Year Staff Questionnaire

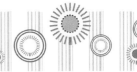

Please answer the following questions in order to help me make this a good teaching year for you. Thank you for your help!

Name: _____

Co-teachers: _____

1 Which age group do you enjoy most? Why?

2 What do you like most about your job?

3 What do you like least about your job?

4 What is the most successful lesson you have ever planned?

5 What are your goals for the school year?

6 Do you have any concerns or worries about the upcoming school year?

7 What questions do you have for me?

8 Do you have any other comments?

End-of-the-Year Staff Questionnaire

Please answer the following questions in order to help me assess the school year and make improvements for next year. Thank you for your help!

Name: _____

Co-teachers: _____

1 What is your best memory from this year?

2 What is your worst memory from this year?

3 What is the best thing that happened as a result of working as part of our school's team?

4 How could the school's team improve the way we work together?

5 What parts of your class lesson plans and ideas worked well this year?

6 What changes would you like to make to your classroom for next year?

7 Do you have any specific materials requests for next year?

8 Do you have any other comments?

Date:

Staff Meeting Planner

Time:	Topic: Notes:
Time:	Topic: Notes:
Time:	Topic: Notes:
Time:	Topic: Notes:
Time:	Topic: Notes:

Purchase Request

_____   _____
Amount Requested   Today's Date

_____   _____
Teacher's Name   Classroom

_____
Item(s) to Be Purchased

_____
Item(s) to Be Purchased

_____
Office/Director Signature

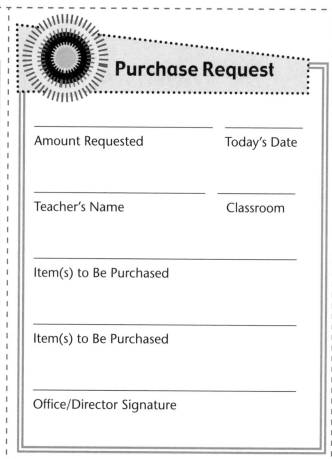

Purchase Request

_____   _____
Amount Requested   Today's Date

_____   _____
Teacher's Name   Classroom

_____
Item(s) to Be Purchased

_____
Item(s) to Be Purchased

_____
Office/Director Signature

Reimbursement Form

_____   _____
Amount Requested   Today's Date

_____   _____
Your Name   Phone No.

_____
Reason for Purchase

**PLEASE STAPLE THIS COMPLETED FORM
TO YOUR RECEIPTS.**

_____   _____
Date of Reimbursement   Staff Initials

Reimbursement Form

_____   _____
Amount Requested   Today's Date

_____   _____
Your Name   Phone No.

_____
Reason for Purchase

**PLEASE STAPLE THIS COMPLETED FORM
TO YOUR RECEIPTS.**

_____   _____
Date of Reimbursement   Staff Initials

Sample Director's Daily Schedule

Preschool and day-care directors often find that their day is determined by whatever interruptions occur. A plan to work quietly in your office to catch up on payroll can quickly be changed when a student or teacher or parent needs your help. Use this sample schedule to help you plan your work throughout the day—even if your day does not include thirteen hours, as this one does! Notice that there is office time built into each day, as well as time spent with visitors, inside classrooms, and helping with transitions. Consider trying to build your schedule in a similar fashion so that teachers know approximately where to find you during each day. See page 28 for a blank schedule.

Director's Daily Schedule Planner

Time	Activity	Time	Activity
6:00–6:30	Open the building.	12:30–1:00	Eat lunch.
6:30–7:00	Check e-mail & phone messages.	1:00–1:30	Assist with afternoon pickup.
7:00–7:30	Greet students as they enter building.	1:30–2:00	Review morning classroom observations. Write up report for staff.
7:30–8:00	Check on each classroom. Any special needs?	2:00–2:30	Give prospective parent tour. (Felicia and Darryl Hairston and Ian)
8:00–8:30	Observe Mrs. Branson's & Mrs. Kennedy's classrooms.	2:30–3:00	
8:30–9:00		3:00–3:30	Check e-mail & messages. Work on budget and next week's schedule.
9:00–9:30	Interview applicant for toddler class assistant position. (Nyla Rounds)	3:30–4:00	
9:30–10:00		4:00–4:30	Check on classrooms and help with afternoon snack.
10:00–10:30	Help with morning snack.	4:30–5:00	Finish office work and update incoming evening supervisor.
10:30–11:00	Check e-mail & phone messages.	5:00–5:30	
11:00–11:30	Meet with Jan Reeves about staff CPR training and flu procedures.	5:30–6:00	
11:30–12:00		6:00–6:30	
12:00–12:30	Help with lunch.	6:30–7:00	

See page 27 for a sample schedule.

Director's Daily Schedule Planner

6:00–6:30		**12:30–1:00**	
6:30–7:00		**1:00–1:30**	
7:00–7:30		**1:30–2:00**	
7:30–8:00		**2:00–2:30**	
8:00–8:30		**2:30–3:00**	
8:30–9:00		**3:00–3:30**	
9:00–9:30		**3:30–4:00**	
9:30–10:00		**4:00–4:30**	
10:00–10:30		**4:30–5:00**	
10:30–11:00		**5:00–5:30**	
11:00–11:30		**5:30–6:00**	
11:30–12:00		**6:00–6:30**	
12:00–12:30		**6:30–7:00**	

DIRECTOR EVALUATION FORM

DIRECTOR'S NAME: _____ DATE: _____

For each category, circle the number that best applies. The highest possible score is 5.

MANAGEMENT STYLE

Is well prepared for each day.	1	2	3	4	5
Schedule is flexible; accommodates needs of students, parents, and staff.	1	2	3	4	5
Keeps parents, teachers, and other staff aware of schedule and school events.	1	2	3	4	5
Communicates needs of staff and facility to upper management and parents.	1	2	3	4	5
Willingly mentors new staff members.	1	2	3	4	5
Fairly distributes classroom supplies and resources.	1	2	3	4	5
Is flexible and willing to help out in other areas as needed.	1	2	3	4	5
Follows absence and vacation policies.	1	2	3	4	5
Builds a positive working environment at facility.	1	2	3	4	5
Clearly expresses expectations of staff.	1	2	3	4	5
Regularly observes classroom teachers and gives timely job performance reviews.	1	2	3	4	5
Clearly advises staff about strengths and weaknesses of their job performances.	1	2	3	4	5
Maintains confidentiality with staff.	1	2	3	4	5
Treats staff with respect.	1	2	3	4	5

INTERACTIONS WITH STUDENTS AND PARENTS

Greets students and parents by first name.	1	2	3	4	5
Interacts well with students and parents.	1	2	3	4	5
Responds to parents' concerns promptly and professionally.	1	2	3	4	5
Creates positive solutions to problems as they arise.	1	2	3	4	5
Communicates effectively with parents on a regular basis.	1	2	3	4	5
Offers conference times as needed.	1	2	3	4	5
Maintains confidentiality with parents.	1	2	3	4	5

STAFF MEMBER DEVELOPMENT

Holds regular staff meetings.	1	2	3	4	5
Ensures that all staff have completed CPR and first-aid training.	1	2	3	4	5
Offers opportunities for staff to accumulate required development hours.	1	2	3	4	5
Stays up-to-date with child development theory and practice.	1	2	3	4	5
Relays information on child development theory and practice to staff.	1	2	3	4	5

FACILITY MANAGEMENT

Facility is clean and inviting.	1	2	3	4	5
Facility is safe and accessible for all students.	1	2	3	4	5
Developmentally appropriate materials and furniture are provided.	1	2	3	4	5
Outdoor play areas are contained, safe, and age appropriate.	1	2	3	4	5
Students' nutritional needs are met as appropriate for facility and operating hours.	1	2	3	4	5
Custodial services are satisfactory.	1	2	3	4	5
Safe, organized child pickup and drop-off systems are in place.	1	2	3	4	5
Funds for budget and payroll are organized and properly allocated.	1	2	3	4	5
Expenses are properly documented.	1	2	3	4	5

EVALUATOR'S COMMENTS

DIRECTOR'S COMMENTS

GOALS ACCOMPLISHED (See previous evaluation from _____.)
Date

NEW GOALS SET (See previous evaluation from _____.)
Date

EVALUATOR'S SIGNATURE: _____ DATE: _____

DIRECTOR'S SIGNATURE: _____ DATE: _____

Parent Tour Checklist

Date: _____ Time: _____

Introductions (director, office staff, parents)

__ Parents' names: _____
__ Students' names and ages:_____
__ Classes requested: _____
__ Review preschool information (brochure, registration form, accreditation information).
__ Distribute visitor's pass if needed.

Classroom Visit

__ Introduce teachers.
__ Spend time in classroom and tour other areas child will be using.
__ Allow time for parents to ask questions.

Follow-Up

__ Return to office for additional questions.
__ Give parents your contact information.
__ Follow up with a phone call within four days.

Parent Tour Checklist

Date: _____ Time: _____

Introductions (director, office staff, parents)

__ Parents' names: _____
__ Students' names and ages:_____
__ Classes requested: _____
__ Review preschool information (brochure, registration form, accreditation information).
__ Distribute visitor's pass if needed.

Classroom Visit

__ Introduce teachers.
__ Spend time in classroom and tour other areas child will be using.
__ Allow time for parents to ask questions.

Follow-Up

__ Return to office for additional questions.
__ Give parents your contact information.
__ Follow up with a phone call within four days.

Date: _____

Parent Survey

Dear Parents,

Below is a brief survey about your impressions of our preschool program. Please take a few minutes to complete the survey and return it to the school. We appreciate your feedback and suggestions for making our program the best it can be.

Parent and Child/Children's Names (optional): _____

For each category, circle the number that best applies. The highest possible score is 5.

Facility

Facility is clean and inviting.	1 2 3 4 5
Facility is safe and accessible for all children.	1 2 3 4 5
Developmentally appropriate materials and furniture are provided.	1 2 3 4 5
Outdoor play areas are contained, safe, and age appropriate.	1 2 3 4 5
Children's nutritional needs are met as appropriate.	1 2 3 4 5
Custodial services are satisfactory.	1 2 3 4 5
Safe, organized child pickup and drop-off procedures are in place.	1 2 3 4 5

Staff Interactions with Parents and Children

My child and I are greeted by a staff member each day.	1 2 3 4 5
A staff member says goodbye to my child and me each day.	1 2 3 4 5
My child's teacher seems happy to see my child.	1 2 3 4 5
I feel confident that my child is well cared for each day.	1 2 3 4 5
The teachers and staff keep me apprised of daily schedules and school events.	1 2 3 4 5
My child and I are treated with kindness and respect.	1 2 3 4 5
The school handbook and other rules are sensible and easy to follow.	1 2 3 4 5
Teachers and staff maintain confidentiality when appropriate.	1 2 3 4 5

Curriculum

Classroom activities are enjoyable for my child.	1 2 3 4 5
Classroom activities seem age appropriate for my child.	1 2 3 4 5
I see my child's work and projects.	1 2 3 4 5
My child's learning needs are being met in this classroom.	1 2 3 4 5
I am aware of my child's progress toward learning and developmental goals.	1 2 3 4 5
My child's teachers update me regularly through progress reports.	1 2 3 4 5
My child's teachers are available for conferences.	1 2 3 4 5

Comments

Meeting Feedback Form

Attendee's Name (optional): _____

Meeting Attended: _____

Date: _____

For each category, circle the number that best applies. The highest possible score is 5.

I received adequate notice prior to the meeting.   1 2 3 4 5

The meeting started and ended on time.   1 2 3 4 5

The meeting topic was interesting and informative.   1 2 3 4 5

It was easy to understand the speaker.   1 2 3 4 5

I would like to attend more meetings like this one.   1 2 3 4 5

Something I learned from this meeting:

A suggestion I have for a future meeting topic is:

Meeting Feedback Form

Attendee's Name (optional): _____

Meeting Attended: _____

Date: _____

For each category, circle the number that best applies. Numeral 5 is the highest possible score.

I received adequate notice prior to the meeting.   1 2 3 4 5

The meeting started and ended on time.   1 2 3 4 5

The meeting topic was interesting and informative.   1 2 3 4 5

It was easy to understand the speaker.   1 2 3 4 5

I would like to attend more meetings like this one.   1 2 3 4 5

Something I learned from this meeting:

A suggestion I have for a future meeting topic is:

FUND-RAISER & EVENT SUMMARY

Use this form to help you evaluate the success of your fund-raiser or special event and summarize important details for the next chairperson.

Name of fund-raiser: _____

Date of fund-raiser: _____

Chairperson/Cochairs:_____

Other volunteers:_____

_____

Cost to put on event: _____

Gross (money before expenses) raised:_____

Net (money after expenses) raised: _____

INFORMATION FOR NEXT CHAIRPERSON

Important contacts and phone numbers: _____

_____

_____

Other useful information:_____

_____

_____

_____

_____

_____

_____

_____

_____

VOLUNTEERS NEEDED!

Dear Parents,

Below we have listed some events and projects that require extra parental involvement. We need your help! Please sign up for anything you can assist with and please complete one form per family. Thank you in advance for your willingness to serve.

YOUR NAME: _____

Phone: _____ E-mail: _____

CHILD'S NAME(S)/TEACHER(S):

1) _____

2) _____

3) _____

EVENT: _____ **DATE:** _____

___ I will help with _____

___ I will help with _____

___ I will help with _____

___ I will help with _____

EVENT: _____ **DATE:** _____

___ I will help with _____

___ I will help with _____

___ I will help with _____

___ I will help with _____

EVENT: _____ **DATE:** _____

___ I will help with _____

___ I will help with _____

___ I will help with _____

___ I will help with _____

Essential Topics for Staff/Parent Orientation

When planning a parent or teacher meeting at the beginning of the year, use this form to make sure you have covered all of the bases.

___ Welcome

___ Description of the program (kind of program, mission statement, philosophies that guide the program)

___ Introductions (old and new staff, other meeting attendees)

___ Contact information (address, phone number, Web site, e-mail)

___ School-wide policies and procedures—need to be relayed to staff (Some will be passed on to parents.)

- school hours
- security codes
- inclement weather procedures
- holidays and days off
- sick leave and vacation day policies
- pay schedule for teachers and/or students
- staff medical forms
- registration procedures and policies
- late fee policies

- withdrawal policies
- drop-off and pickup procedures
- cleaning guidelines
- classroom setup standards
- playground procedures
- field trip guidelines and procedures
- emergency and security procedures
- snack and lunch schedules
- discipline policies

___ Classroom policies and procedures—need to be relayed to staff and parents

- teacher qualifications
- child/adult ratios
- curriculum
- visitor policies
- class parties
- toilet-training requirements
- medical forms

- immunization requirements
- parent volunteer organizations
- newsletters
- conferences
- progress reports
- classroom supplies needed

___ Orientation schedule

___ Staff-to-parent mailings

___ Upcoming staff development hours

___ Schedule of staff meetings and topics for the year

___ Team-building activity (See next page for examples.)

Team-Building Activities for Teachers, Parents & Children

Teachers

- Have a staff member tell something that she admires about the way a fellow staff member does her job. That staff member must then choose someone else to compliment. Continue until everyone has had a turn.

- Use this as a simple get-to-know-you activity. Let teachers group themselves in different ways. For example, have them move into groups according to birth months, number of children, hair color, etc. Let them remain and chat in the group for five minutes and then change groups. This works for older preschoolers and for parents, too!

- A grown-up version of "Telephone" is a team-building activity that can show how gossip affects the workplace. Start a rumor at the beginning of the meeting. Charge the person who hears it to add to the gossip and tell one person at some point during the meeting. That person should tell someone else, and so on. Compare the original to the final rumor to demonstrate how easy it is to spread untrue information.

- At Thanksgiving or at a regular staff meeting, post a blank sheet of bulletin board paper. Encourage teachers to write messages about why they are thankful for each other. Place no limit on postings. It's a great way to spread good news and appreciation among staff.

Parents

- Use the "Playing in My Favorite Place" game to find out more about parents. Write the name of each center on a separate sheet of paper. Post the sheets in their corresponding centers. Be sure to include one at the door for the playground. Ask parents to go to their favorite centers. Have them answer these questions: What do you see in this center? Why do you like this center? What makes you want to stay here? What will you play with first? What else do you wish was in this center? After the activity, chart the results. This will show you something about parents, and it will also give you different perspectives about your centers. Parents can do this activity with their older preschool children as well. And, even teachers can do it—you will find out about their favorites.

- Play "Teacher, Teacher!" Give parents a chance to put you on the spot. Ask each parent to send in a question for you ahead of time. When you have a parent meeting or orientation, read the questions aloud and answer them. For extra fun, have them send in questions from their children.

Children

- Host a scavenger hunt to familiarize students with the classroom. Make a picture list that instructs them to find things such as their cubbies, the bathroom, the art closet, the first letters in their names, and one particular classmate each. Have them introduce their classmates at the end of the scavenger hunt. (Remember to provide help with reading as needed.) Use the **"Come Meet My Friends" Scavenger Hunt** (page 79) for inspiration.

FORMS FOR THE OFFICE STAFF

The office staff may choose forms from this section to make sure student paperwork is up-to-date and as streamlined as possible.

The **School Registration/Application Form** (page 39) is the sheet parents will fill out to register their children for preschool or child care. Each student must have a separate form in the office file. When a child has been accepted into the program, the office staff should mail a **Registration Confirmation** (page 40) confirming the child's enrollment. This lets parents know that a place has been saved for their child. The notification also serves as the first tuition reminder for parents. If it is necessary to communicate with certain parents who are late in paying the tuition, send a completed **Tuition Payment Reminder** (page 41) to them. The **Student Background Information** sheet (pages 42 and 43) gathers pertinent information about each child at the start of the school year. This form is useful because it alerts teachers to each child's special interests and needs. (Except for the Tuition Payment Reminder, all of these forms need to be completed annually.)

Parents should fill out all medical forms, including the **Student Medical Form** (page 44), which must also be signed by the child's pediatrician; the **Student Emergency Contact Card** (page 45) that lists whom to contact in the event of an emergency; and a **Medication Dispensation Release Form** (page 46) that gives permission to teachers to dispense medicines (a doctor's note is required here). The **Allergy Action Plan** (page 47) alerts teachers to potentially dangerous situations for a child with allergies. It also includes space for parents to provide information about what to do in an allergy emergency. The **Emergency Phone Numbers** (page 48) should be posted in the office and in every classroom.

The office staff will probably need other forms throughout the year to help manage teachers' tasks. Once all of the students have been confirmed for the school year, fill out the **Classroom Assignment Sheet** (page 49) to assign children to classrooms. The **Teacher Profile** (page 50) will be helpful for parents who like to provide treats for teachers. Also included in this section is a generic **Budget Worksheet** (page 51) to help office staff, directors, or teachers plan their budgets. If your facility does not have a food or paper products service, use the **Shopping Checklist** (page 52) to simplify shopping trips for snacks, art materials, cleaning supplies, paper products, and so on.

> ● GOOD IDEA! ●
>
> Have all teachers fill out a new Teacher Profile at the beginning of each school year. Keep the profiles in a notebook in the office for parents and fellow teachers to browse.

Keep other administrative needs simple with these forms, including a **Carpool Form** (page 53) that parents can fill out and turn in to alert you to children sharing rides. The **Lunch Bunch Tickets** (page 54), and **You Forgot Your Lunch Bunch Ticket** (page 55) cards are provided for those situations, for example, when parents allow their children to stay for lunch and for the occasions when they forget to pay.

Keep up with special event communication using the **Please Come to Our Holiday Program** flier (page 56) and the **School Newsletter Header Templates** (page 57). All of these forms can be modified to suit the needs of any preschool or child-care facility.

School Registration/Application Form

Student Information

Child's full name: _____

Name child is called: _____ Circle one: male   female

Birth date: _____ Age child will be on first day of school: _____

Primary address: _____

City: _____ Zip: _____

Home phone: _____

Family Information

Mother's name: _____

Mother's home phone: _____ Mother's cell phone: _____

Employer: _____ Work phone: _____

Mother's e-mail address: _____

Father's name: _____

Father's home phone: _____ Father's cell phone: _____

Employer: _____ Work phone: _____

Father's e-mail address: _____

Circle: Mother Father   Address (if different from above): _____

_____

Siblings and ages: _____

Emergency Information

Child's physician: _____ Phone: _____

Known allergies: _____

Others to contact in emergency if parents cannot be reached:

1. _____ Phone: _____ Relationship: _____

2. _____ Phone: _____ Relationship: _____

I give permission for emergency treatment if parents cannot be reached.

Parent's signature: _____ Date: _____

Registration Confirmation

Dear _____ ,

Thank you for registering your child for our program. Your child is enrolled in the _____ class for the _____ – _____ school year. We have a record of receiving your registration fee in the amount of _____. Your first tuition payment of _____ is due on _____.

Please sign and return the bottom of form.

I understand that if the first tuition payment is not received by _____ , I forfeit my child's reserved place.

_____   _____
Parent's signature *Date*

Registration Confirmation

Dear _____ ,

Thank you for registering your child for our program. Your child is enrolled in the _____ class for the _____ – _____ school year. We have a record of receiving your registration fee in the amount of _____. Your first tuition payment of _____ is due on _____.

Please sign and return the bottom of form.

I understand that if the first tuition payment is not received by _____ , I forfeit my child's reserved place.

_____   _____
Parent's signature *Date*

$ Tuition Payment Reminder

Dear _____ ,

Your child's tuition is _____ overdue. Currently, you owe _____

for tuition. Please submit payment to us by _____. If you have any questions

or would like to discuss options for payment, please call _____ at

_____ by _____. Thank you.

Sincerely,

_____   _____
Signature   *Date*

- -

$ Tuition Payment Reminder

Dear _____ ,

Your child's tuition is _____ overdue. Currently, you owe _____

for tuition. Please submit payment to us by _____. If you have any questions

or would like to discuss options for payment, please call _____ at

_____ by _____. Thank you.

Sincerely,

_____   _____
Signature   *Date*

Student Background Information

Child's full name:_____

Name child is called:_____ Circle one: male female

Birth date:_____ Age child will be on first day of school: _____

Primary address: _____

City:_____ Zip: _____

Home phone:_____

Family Information

Mother's name:_____

Mother's home phone:_____ Mother's cell phone: _____

Employer:_____ Work phone:_____

Mother's e-mail address: _____

Father's name:_____

Father's home phone:_____ Father's cell phone: _____

Employer: _____ Work phone:_____

Father's e-mail address: _____

Are both parents in the home? ____ If not, which parent is the primary caregiver?_____

Circle: Mother Father Address (if different from above): _____

_____

Siblings and ages:_____

Are there other family members living in the home? _____ If so, please list names, ages, and

relationship to child: _____

Other Personal Information

Is your child toilet trained? ____ Describe assistance needed: _____

_____

Does your child nap? _____ How long?_____

Child's bedtime:_____ Child's wake-up time:_____

Does your child take any medication regularly? _____ Please list medications, dosages,

and times: _____

Does your child have any allergies?_____

Does your child have any health problems (mental, physical, or emotional) of which we should be aware? _____

_____

Please list any serious accidents or surgeries your child has had: _____

_____

Please list any concerns you have about your child's development: _____

_____

Does your child have any problems with vision, hearing, or speech? _____ If so, please explain: _____

Do you feel your child's speech is clear?_____

Do others understand your child when he or she speaks? _____

Help Us Get to Know Your Child

Please list any pets your child has:_____

What are your child's favorite activities?_____

_____

What does your child enjoy doing with Mom? _____

What does your child enjoy doing with Dad? _____

Does your child play well alone?_____ In groups? _____

Are there any neighborhood playmates? What ages?_____

What are your child's favorite TV shows? _____

What behavior control do you use with your child?_____

_____

Has your child been cared for by someone other than immediate family? If so, who and how often? _____

Has your child previously attended another preschool or child-care facility?_____

Please list three words that describe your child: _____

What do you hope your child will learn in preschool this year?_____

_____

Parent's signature:_____ Date: _____

Student Medical Form

● Child's full name: _____

Birth date:_____ Today's date:_____

Name of parent or guardian:_____

Primary address:_____

City:_____ Zip:_____

1 List any previous hospitalizations, significant illnesses, or surgeries:_____

_____

_____

2 Describe any allergies your child has: _____

_____

_____

3 Describe any other conditions that require special attention by staff: _____

_____

_____

4 If any condition is present, describe special care needed: _____

_____

_____

5 List any medications your child must take regularly:_____

_____

_____

YOUR CHILD MUST HAVE HAD A PHYSICAL EXAM PERFORMED BY A LICENSED PHYSICIAN WITHIN THE PAST YEAR.*

Date exam complete: _____ Physician's signature: _____

● Physician's office address and phone number:_____

_____

* PHYSICIAN: PLEASE ATTACH A COPY OF THIS CHILD'S FULL IMMUNIZATION RECORDS. THANK YOU.

STUDENT EMERGENCY CONTACT CARD

Name: _____

Address (Number & Street): _____

City: _____ State: _____ Zip: _____

Home Phone: _____ Parent's Cell Phone: _____

Parent E-mail Address: _____

EMERGENCY CONTACTS

1. Name: _____ Relationship to Student: _____

   Home Number: _____ Cell Number: _____

2. Name: _____ Relationship to Student: _____

   Home Number: _____ Cell Number: _____

Hospital Preference: _____

Primary Physician: _____ Phone: _____

Allergies and Other Medical Concerns (See back of card)

Parent's Signature: _____ Date: _____

- -

STUDENT EMERGENCY CONTACT CARD

Name: _____

Address (Number & Street): _____

City: _____ State: _____ Zip: _____

Home Phone: _____ Parent's Cell Phone: _____

Parent E-mail Address: _____

EMERGENCY CONTACTS

1. Name: _____ Relationship to Student: _____

   Home Number: _____ Cell Number: _____

2. Name: _____ Relationship to Student: _____

   Home Number: _____ Cell Number: _____

Hospital Preference: _____

Primary Physician: _____ Phone: _____

Allergies and Other Medical Concerns (See back of card)

Parent's Signature: _____ Date: _____

Medication Dispensation Release Form

I, _____ , authorize my child's teacher or a staff member
   Parent's or Guardian's name

to give my child, _____ , the following medication(s).
                        Child's name

Medicine: _____   Dosage: _____   Time of Dosage: _____

Medicine: _____   Dosage: _____   Time of Dosage: _____

Medicine: _____   Dosage: _____   Time of Dosage: _____

PLEASE ATTACH A DOCTOR'S NOTE TO AUTHORIZE
DISPENSATION OF PRESCRIPTION MEDICINES.

_____   _____
   Parent's or Guardian's signature   *Date*

Medication Dispensation Release Form

I, _____ , authorize my child's teacher or a staff member
   Parent's or Guardian's name

to give my child, _____ , the following medication(s).
                        Child's name

Medicine: _____   Dosage: _____   Time of Dosage: _____

Medicine: _____   Dosage: _____   Time of Dosage: _____

Medicine: _____   Dosage: _____   Time of Dosage: _____

PLEASE ATTACH A DOCTOR'S NOTE TO AUTHORIZE
DISPENSATION OF PRESCRIPTION MEDICINES.

_____   _____
   Parent's or Guardian's signature   *Date*

Allergy Action Plan

Child's name: _____ Birth date: _____

Teacher's name: _____

Allergic to: _____

Parents' names: _____

Home phone: _____ Cell phone: _____ Work phone: _____

Child's physician: _____ Phone: _____

Describe how your child reacts to exposure to particular allergens:

_____

_____

_____

ACTION PLAN FOR MILD ALLERGIC REACTION

If child exhibits mild symptoms such as _____ ,

administer _____ (amount) of _____ medicine.

Call parent? Yes / No_____ Call physician? Yes / No

Notes: _____

_____

If after 10 minutes, the condition does not improve or worsens,
follow the action plan for severe allergic reaction below.

ACTION PLAN FOR SEVERE ALLERGIC REACTION

If child exhibits severe symptoms such as _____ ,

administer _____ (amount) of _____ medicine immediately.

Epi Pen®? Yes / No   Call 911 immediately. Call parents next. Call physician after parents.

Notes: _____

_____

Parent's signature: _____ Date: _____

Doctor's signature: _____ Date: _____

EMERGENCY PHONE NUMBERS

Call 911 for medical and fire dispatch!

Fill in all pertinent phone numbers and other information.

1 2 3 4 5 6 7 8 9 0

FIRE DEPARTMENT	POLICE DEPARTMENT	LOCAL HOSPITAL
LOCAL MEDICAL CLINIC	POISON CONTROL CENTER	DIRECTOR'S HOME PHONE
DIRECTOR'S CELL PHONE	STAFF MEMBERS TRAINED IN CPR	OTHER NUMBERS

PRESCHOOL/CHILD-CARE FACILITY ADDRESS   **PHONE NUMBER**

Classroom Assignment Chart

Class Name: _____

Teachers: _____

Student's Name	Birth Date	Registration Fee Paid?
_____	_____	_____
_____	_____	_____
_____	_____	_____
_____	_____	_____
_____	_____	_____
_____	_____	_____
_____	_____	_____
_____	_____	_____
_____	_____	_____
_____	_____	_____
_____	_____	_____
_____	_____	_____
_____	_____	_____
_____	_____	_____
_____	_____	_____
_____	_____	_____
_____	_____	_____
_____	_____	_____
_____	_____	_____
_____	_____	_____

Waiting List

_____	_____	_____
_____	_____	_____
_____	_____	_____

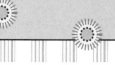

Teacher Profile

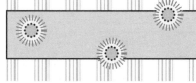
Teacher name

Class

School year

Favorite holiday	
Favorite beverage	
Favorite snack	
Favorite restaurants	
Favorite meal	
Favorite stores	
Favorite things to read	
Favorite ways to relax	
Pets	
Hobbies	
Collections	

Birthday (m/d)

BUDGET WORKSHEET

Total Annual Estimated Spending Budget: _____

Current Month: _____

Remaining Money in Budget: _____

Items to Be Purchased	Estimated Cost

Estimated Total Cost: _____

Budget Prior to Expenses: _____

—

Less Estimated Total Cost: _____

Amount Remaining in Budget: _____

SHOPPING CHECKLIST

Art Supplies
___ Beads (kind: _____

_____)

___ Buttons

___ Chalk

___ Chenille craft stems

___ Child scissors

___ Construction paper

___ Craft sticks

___ Crayons

___ Easel paper

___ Feathers

___ Finger paint paper

___ Foam shapes (kind:

_____)

___ Glitter

___ Glitter glue

___ Glue sticks

___ Paint (kind: _____

_____)

___ Paint cups

___ Paintbrushes

___ Poster board

___ Stickers

___ Tissue paper

___ Washable markers

___ Wiggly eyes

___ Other: _____

___ Other: _____

___ Other: _____

Cleaning Supplies
___ Antibacterial spray

___ Bleach

___ Cleaning wipes

___ Floor cleaner

___ General cleaner

___ Glass cleaner

___ Hand soap

___ Hand wipes

___ Toilet cleaner

___ Vinegar

___ Other: _____

___ Other: _____

___ Other: _____

Miscellaneous
___ Baking soda

___ Batteries

___ Disposable cameras

___ Camera digital card

___ Film

___ Hook-and-loop tape

___ Trash bags

___ Other: _____

___ Other: _____

___ Other: _____

Office Supplies
___ Binder clips

___ Brads

___ Butcher paper

___ Copier paper

___ Colorful copier paper

___ Envelopes

___ File folders

___ Glue

___ Liquid eraser

___ Paper clips

___ Pencils

___ Pens

___ Permanent markers

___ Poster board

___ Scissors

___ Stamps

___ Staples

___ Tape

___ Other: _____

___ Other: _____

___ Other: _____

Paper Products
___ Bathroom tissue

___ Drinking straws

___ Food service gloves

___ Napkins

___ Paper cups

___ Paper plates

___ Paper towels

___ Plastic bags

___ Plastic cutlery

___ Other: _____

___ Other: _____

___ Other: _____

Snack Foods
___ Apples

___ Applesauce

___ Bananas

___ Cereal (kinds: _____

_____

_____)

___ Cereal bars

___ Cheese

___ Cheese crackers

___ Crackers (kinds: _____

_____

_____)

___ Fish crackers

___ Graham crackers

___ Mini-muffins

___ Pretzels

___ Vanilla wafers

___ Yogurt

___ Other: _____

___ Other: _____

___ Other: _____

Special Notes

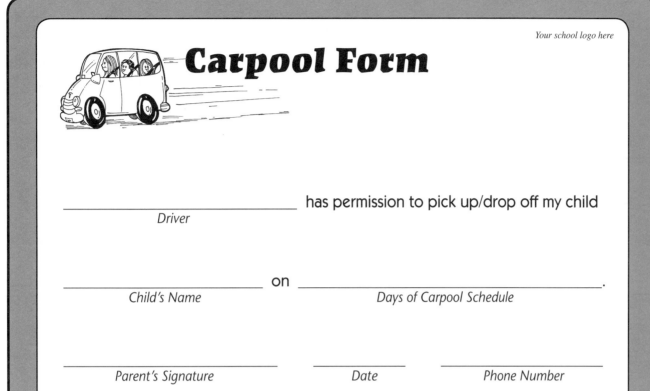

Carpool Form

_____ has permission to pick up/drop off my child
Driver

_____ on _____.
Child's Name   **Days of Carpool Schedule**

_____   _____   _____
Parent's Signature   **Date**   **Phone Number**

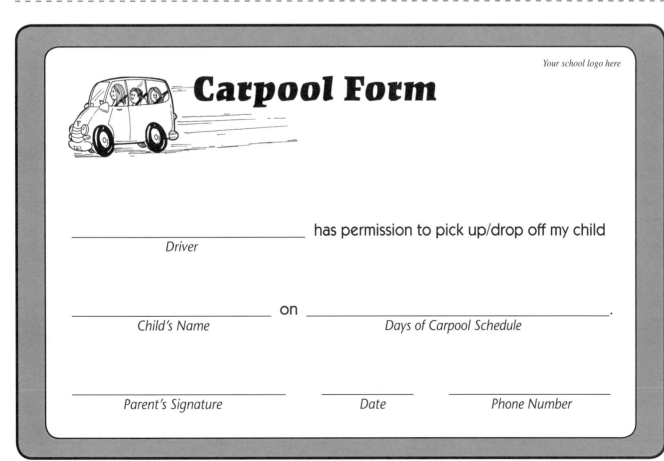

Carpool Form

_____ has permission to pick up/drop off my child
Driver

_____ on _____.
Child's Name   **Days of Carpool Schedule**

_____   _____   _____
Parent's Signature   **Date**   **Phone Number**

Lunch Bunch Tickets

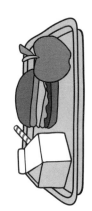  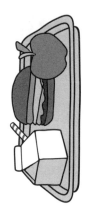

is staying for lunch today!

is staying for lunch today!

is staying for lunch today!

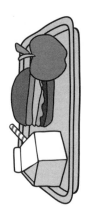

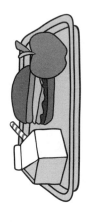 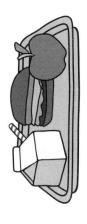

is staying for lunch today!

is staying for lunch today!

is staying for lunch today!

  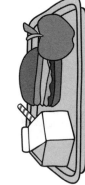

is staying for lunch today!

is staying for lunch today!

is staying for lunch today!

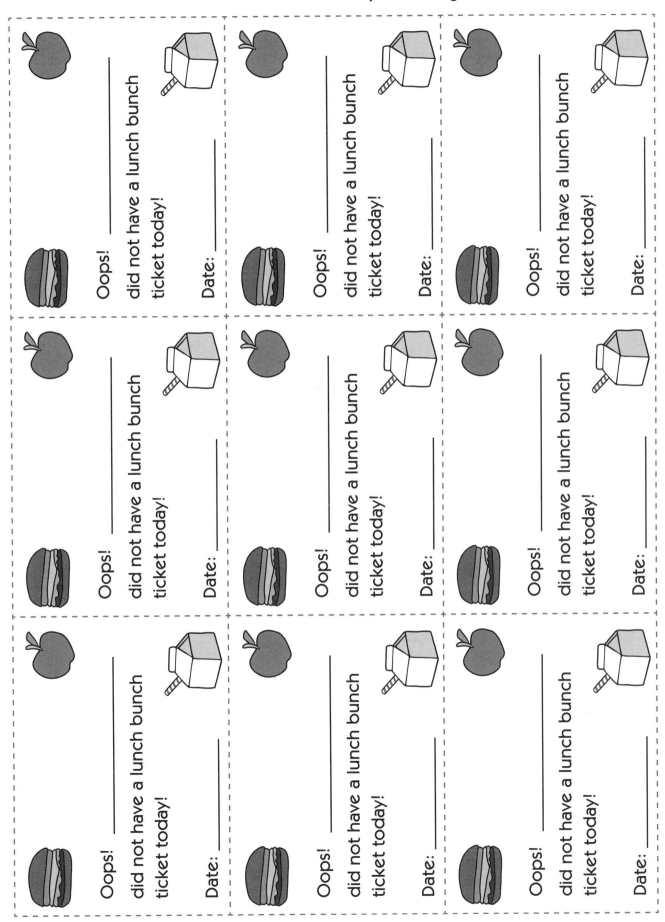

Oops! _____
did not have a lunch bunch
ticket today!

Date: _____

Oops! _____
did not have a lunch bunch
ticket today!

Date: _____

Oops! _____
did not have a lunch bunch
ticket today!

Date: _____

Oops! _____
did not have a lunch bunch
ticket today!

Date: _____

Oops! _____
did not have a lunch bunch
ticket today!

Date: _____

Oops! _____
did not have a lunch bunch
ticket today!

Date: _____

Oops! _____
did not have a lunch bunch
ticket today!

Date: _____

Oops! _____
did not have a lunch bunch
ticket today!

Date: _____

Oops! _____
did not have a lunch bunch
ticket today!

Date: _____

Please come to our _____ **program**
to see your child perform.

Date _____   **Time** _____

Place _____

Schedule of Events

Special Notes

Please come to our _____ **program**
to see your child perform.

Date _____   **Time** _____

Place _____

Schedule of Events

Special Notes

Program header template with name of month.

_____ SCHOOL NEWSLETTER

_____ Newsletter

_____ Newsletter

_____ Newsletter

_____ Newsletter   Date: _____

FORMS FOR TEACHERS TO USE

Whether or not your preschool or day-care facility uses a standard curriculum, it helps to document many different things carefully in the classroom. If you systematically record students' behavior and development, you can easily see in which skill areas some children are progressing and others are struggling. You can also plan lessons and themes and detail classroom needs, successes, and failures.

Every classroom needs a **Class Roster** (page 60) for a quick reference. After you fill it out, copy it to send to parents. It will help them get to know their child's friends more quickly. To make the **Daily Attendance Form** (page 61) look seasonal, just select one of the borders in Chapter 6 and use it to decorate a reduced copy of the chart.

It's hard to find time to make thorough observations during the school day, so jot down your comments on a **Quick Observation** form (pages 62 and 63). One form is offered for the skill development of infants and toddlers and the other focuses on children ages two through five. For a more thorough list of observations, fill out a **Progress Checklist** (pages 64–66). These are forms that reference what is developmentally appropriate for infants, toddlers and two-year-olds, and three- to five-year-olds. You can use the information from the Observation and Checklist forms to prepare for your conferences by filling out the **Progress Report for Parent-Teacher Conference** (page 67). Send a copy of the completed form with parents and keep one for each child's file.

The **Classroom Arrangement Evaluation** form (page 68) can be used at the beginning of the school year to design your furniture and centers arrangement or throughout the year to evaluate how the room is set up. For those teachers who

like to plan ahead, the **Weekly Theme Planner** (page 69) and **Lesson Planner** (page 70) help get your thoughts on paper about upcoming units and the lessons for those designated units. (For more writing space, enlarge the Theme Planner to fit 11" x 14" paper.) Use these planners in conjunction with the **Theme Box Supply List** (page 71). Fill out this list to keep track of supplies that are used during a particular unit of study. Finally, the **Please Share with Me!** form (page 72) can be posted in the staff room to ask fellow teachers to share their supplies to supplement your current class theme.

Daily tasks are addressed in this chapter with a **"Used the Potty!" Incentive Chart** (page 73) for when a child is being toilet trained and a set of pictures titled **Wash Your Hands!** (pages 74 and 75) that stresses the proper procedure as children get clean. Directions for making a poster on a file folder are included with the patterns.

◉ GOOD IDEA! ◉

To get children to wash their hands long enough, purchase self-foaming soap. Have children line up as you squirt soap onto each child's hands. As children rub the soap all over their hands, sing a song that lasts about 15 seconds, such as "Wash, wash, wash your hands, wash them nice and clean. Fronts and backs, fronts and backs, And fingers in between! (Sing to the tune of "Row, Row, Row Your Boat," repeating the verse twice. Consider making up other washing songs to keep children interested.) After singing the verses, have children rinse, dry, and throw away trash—assembly line style.

The following forms are geared toward class guests. One is a **Planner for Substitute** (page 82) that will guide a sub through the day in your classroom. The other is a **Sign-Up Sheet for Parent-Teacher Conferences** (page 83). First, label the form with dates and times when you are available. Then, post it outside of your classroom door so that parents can choose the best times for them to meet with you.

◉ GOOD IDEA! ◉

For students with nontraditional families, simply alter the parent questionnaires to include another favorite family member.

The **Look Whose Birthday It Is!** chart (page 76) can serve as a handy reminder when filling out calendars, making the birthday bulletin-board display, or shopping for party items if you treat students on their birthdays. The completed form can also be posted in a special area for parents to read.

The next set of forms is comprised of well-liked class activities. Students will enjoy dictating their thoughts and creating some drawings for the **All About Me** booklet (pages 77 and 78), a great project to use at the beginning of the year. Parents will get to know their children's classroom better by participating in the **"Come Meet My Friends" Scavenger Hunt** (page 79). Students will enjoy telling all about their parents by answering the interview questions on the **About My Mommy** (page 80) and **About My Daddy** (page 81) questionnaires (see examples).

Class Roster for _____

Child's Name	Parent's Name	Phone Number/E-mail Address

Use one of the borders in Chapter 6 to decorate this form with a seasonal theme.

Daily Attendance Form

for _____ Class

Dates of Week: _____ to _____

Child's Name	Mon.	Tues.	Wed.	Thurs.	Fri.

Notes:

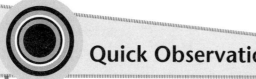

Quick Observation

Infants & Toddlers

Date:

Name:

Time:

Child Observed During . . .
(Circle one.)

- arrival
- circle time
- manipulative area

- playground
- art
- snack
- lunch

- rest time
- center time
- bathroom

Observation:

Comments:

Observed by:

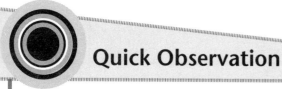

Quick Observation

Infants & Toddlers

Date:

Name:

Time:

Child Observed During . . .
(Circle one.)

- arrival
- circle time
- manipulative area

- playground
- art
- snack
- lunch

- rest time
- center time
- bathroom

Observation:

Comments:

Observed by:

Two- to Five-Year-Olds

Quick Observation

Date:

Name:

Time:

Child Observed During . . .
(Circle one.)

- arrival
- circle time
- manipulative area

- playground
- art
- snack
- lunch

- quiet time
- center time
- transition in classroom

- transition outside of classroom
- bathroom

Observation:

Comments:

Observed by:

Two- to Five-Year-Olds

Quick Observation

Date:

Name:

Time:

Child Observed During . . .
(Circle one.)

- arrival
- circle time
- manipulative area

- playground
- art
- snack
- lunch

- quiet time
- center time
- transition in classroom

- transition outside of classroom
- bathroom

Observation:

Comments:

Observed by:

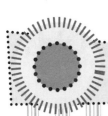

Progress Checklist : Infants

Child's name:

Birth date:

Caregiver's name:

Today's date:

Skills at Three Months	Always	Sometimes	Never
Lifts head and shoulders while on tummy			
Responds to sounds by turning head			
Gurgles and coos			
Makes eye contact			
Follows objects with eyes			
Smiles and laughs			
Recognizes parents and caregivers			
Bears weight on legs			
Stretches legs out and kicks while on tummy or back			
Bats at dangling objects			

Skills at Nine Months	Always	Sometimes	Never
Repeats syllables (ma-ma-ma)			
Passes objects from one hand to the other			
"Sweeps" hand to pick up an object			
Points			
Waves good-bye			
Grasps objects between thumb and first finger			
Crawls			
Stands with support			
Bangs object to make sound			
Responds to his/her first name			

Skills at Six Months	Always	Sometimes	Never
Holds head steadily			
Turns over (eventually in both directions)			
Grasps			
Releases objects			
Plays with own hands and feet			
Responds to talk with cooing and babbling			
Reaches for objects			
Mouths objects			
Sits without support			

Skills at Twelve Months	Always	Sometimes	Never
Makes sounds that are like words (may say words to name objects and people)			
Explores while "cruising" (walking while holding on to furniture)			
Understands "no"			
Puts objects in a container and pours them out			
Plays infant games (peekaboo)			
Stands alone or takes a few steps			
Understands and follows simple instructions			
Can finger feed him/herself			
Pokes things with index finger			
Drops things to see what happens			

Comments

Progress Checklist : Toddlers & Two-Year-Olds

Child's name:	Birth date:
Caregiver's name:	Today's date:

Language & Cognitive Skills	Always	Sometimes	Never
Uses phrases of two words or more			
Responds to instructions			
Uses "No!" & "Mine!"			
Understands at least 200 words			
Points and names objects			
Follows multistep directions			
Talks about self			
Asks, "Why?"			
Speaks clearly most of the time			
Uses pronouns correctly, especially "I"			
Sings songs			
Talks about how to use an object			
Demonstrates understanding of position words			

Gross Motor Skills	Always	Sometimes	Never
Walks well			
Holds out arms or legs to "help" get dressed			
Rolls a ball back and forth to someone			
Pushes and pulls a toy			
Climbs			
Stoops and picks up objects from floor without falling down			
Walks up and down stairs			
Runs			
Can kick a large stationary ball			
Balances on one foot			

Social & Emotional Skills	Always	Sometimes	Never
Expresses food preferences			
Throws a tantrum when frustrated			
Uses objects like a phone, broom, or doll for dramatic play			
Is aware of gender differences			
Plays side-by-side with friends			
Plays with friends			
Can show feelings on command (happy, sad, silly)			

Fine Motor Skills	Always	Sometimes	Never
Drinks from a cup			
Puts on an article of clothing			
Stacks blocks			
Turns pages of a book			
Scribbles with a crayon or pencil			

Comments

Progress Checklist : Three- to Five-Year-Olds

Child's name:

Birth date:

Teacher's name:

Today's date:

Language & Cognitive Skills	Always	Sometimes	Never
Carries on a conversation with another person			
Asks questions			
Follows three-step directions			
Speaks clearly			
Listens carefully			
Can recall a simple story			
Assists in cleanup			
Can stay focused for an appropriate length of time			
Recognizes and names eight basic colors			
Recognizes own name in print			
Can identify 10 letters in isolation, especially those in own name			
Says the alphabet in sequence			
Can identify several numerals			
Can count up to 10 by rote			
Can identify sets of 3+ objects without counting			
Can name basic shapes			
Demonstrates understanding of directionality and position of objects (on top, under, beside, etc.)			
Identifies letters in environmental print			
Reads independently			

Fine Motor Skills	Always	Sometimes	Never
Dresses self			
Buttons, zips, snaps clothing			
Uses scissors correctly			
Holds crayon or pencil correctly			
Writes own name			
Draws simple shapes or pictures			

Social & Emotional Skills	Always	Sometimes	Never
Identifies own gender			
Separates from parents easily			
Takes turns and shares			
Refrains from tantrums			
Plays well in small groups			
Plays well independently			
Shows self-discipline			
Solves simple problems independently			
Uses materials respectfully			

Gross Motor Skills	Always	Sometimes	Never
Walks well			
Runs well			
Opens and closes doors easily			
Hops			
Walks backwards			
Jumps			
Can stop abruptly			
Sits still in a chair			
Marches			
Throws a ball			
Gallops			
Skips			
Can bounce a ball			
Walks up and down stairs by alternating feet			
Can transition between motor skills (e.g., running and jumping)			
Catches a ball			
Pumps legs when swinging			

Comments

Progress Report *for* Parent-Teacher Conference

Child's name:	Birth date:

Social/Emotional:

Examples:

Gross-Motor Skills:

Examples:

Fine-Motor Skills:

Examples:

Cognitive/Language:

Examples:

Self-Help Skills:

Examples:

Developmental Skills Mastered:

Continue to work on . . .

Teacher & Parent Comments:

Teacher's signature:	Date:
Parent's signature:	Date:

Classroom Arrangement Evaluation

Draw a diagram of your classroom. Be sure first to indicate permanent objects like windows, cabinets, shelves, and bathroom locations. Then, use the remaining space to plan the placement of your centers and circle area. Try to keep quiet areas (books, manipulatives, listening center) together and loud areas (blocks, musical instruments, dramatic play, doorway) together.

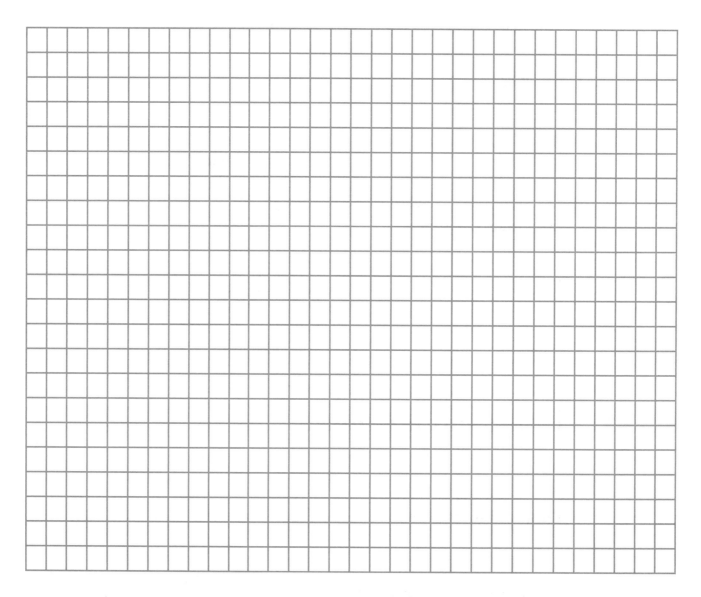

Things to Consider:

- Which centers are working well? Why?

- Which centers are not working well? Why?

- Are any centers going to change with the new theme?

  If so, what are your plans?

- What materials and equipment are needed?

Weekly Theme Planner for Unit on _____

Date: _____

Teachers: _____

Instructional goals:

	Monday	Tuesday	Wednesday	Thursday	Friday
Circle Time					
Story Time					
Transitions					
Outdoors					
Special Events					

At-home activity

Community/Family involvement

Record thematic changes to classroom centers on page 71 and attach it to this sheet.

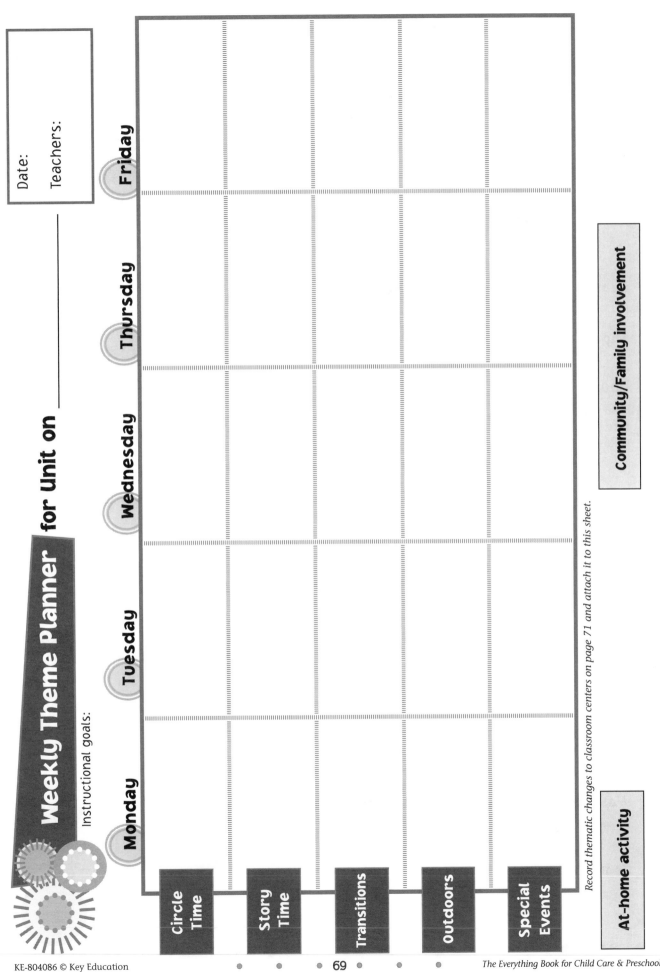

Lesson Planner for

Date

Lesson title:

Teachers:

Goals for the lesson:

Center in which to complete lesson:

Supplies and materials needed:

Books:

Steps for lesson:

1.
2.
3.
4.
5.
6.

Skills taught:

Was this a good lesson? Why or why not?

Changes for next time:

Theme Box Supply List for Unit on

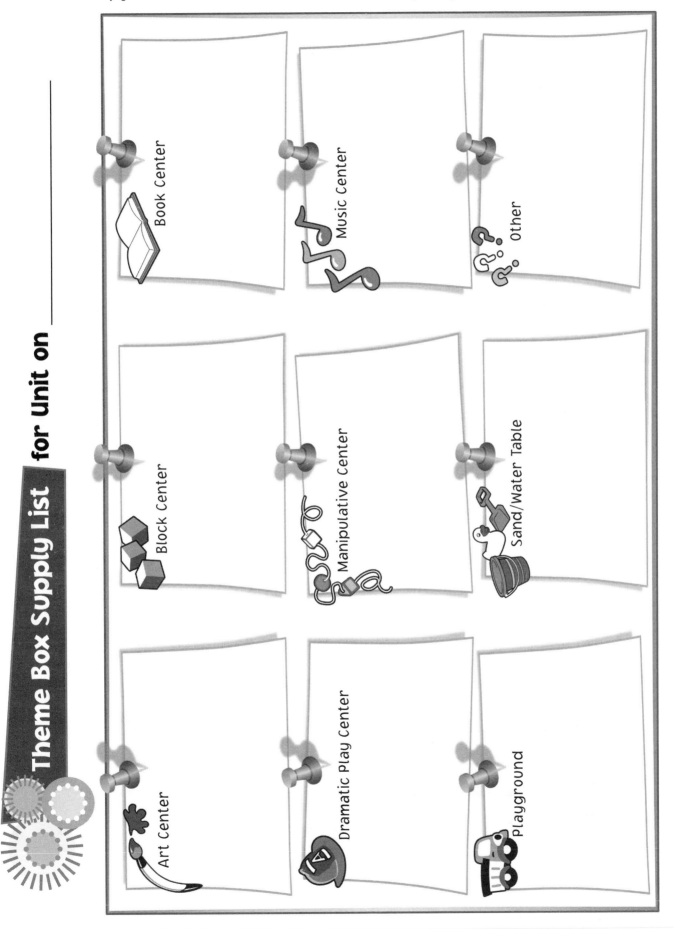

Book Center

Music Center

Other

Block Center

Manipulative Center

Sand/Water Table

Art Center

Dramatic Play Center

Playground

Please Share with Me!

I am planning to do a/an _____ theme

unit in my classroom on _____.

And, I would like to use the following items:

Can you help? Please share the items during this time.

Thanks,

Comments:

If needed, enlarge before making photocopies.

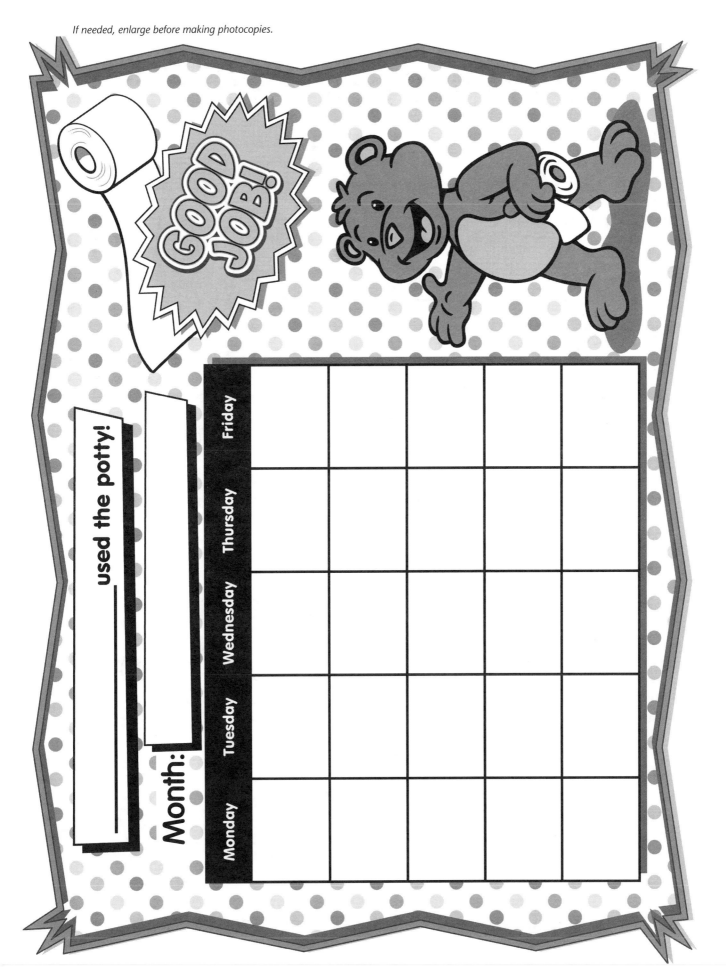

used the potty!

Month:

Monday	Tuesday	Wednesday	Thursday	Friday

Wash Your Hands!

1

Wait for your turn at the sink.

2

Wet your hands.

5

Rinse your hands very well.

6

Dry your hands on a paper towel.

Suggestions
- Prepare a set of picture cards by copying pages 74 and 75 onto card stock. Cut out the cards along the dashed lines.
- Show the children the cards. Make up a simple story about the animals that are depicted on the cards to talk about what is happening in the scenes. Play a game with the pictures. Cover the numbers and then let the children arrange the pictures in the correct order.
- To make a poster, color a set of pictures and then glue them along with the title to the inside panels of a colorful file folder. You may wish to laminate the materials for durability.

Squirt soap on your hand.

Rub soap ALL OVER your hands.

Throw away your paper towel.

Good job!

Look Whose Birthday It Is!

Here is a picture of me.

Name: _____ Today's date is _____.

This is my handprint.

I get bigger every day. My height is _____.

My weight is _____.

-2-

I like . . .

When I grow up, I want to be . . .

-3-

This is me with my family.

-4-

"Come Meet My Friends" Scavenger Hunt

Look for each item with your child. Write your answers on the lines. When you are finished, see the teacher for a surprise!

1. What is your child's favorite play area in the classroom? _____

2. Find your child's artwork. Ask, "What is it?" _____

3. Find the restroom.

4. Where are the crayons stored in the classroom? _____

5. What is in your child's cubby? _____

6. Have your child introduce you to a friend. What is the friend's name? _____

7. Does your child have a job this week? If so, what is it? _____

8. Where can you find the lunch boxes? _____

9. Find the classroom library. Ask, "What is your favorite book?" Record the title.

   _____

10. Find the playground. Ask, "What is your favorite thing to do here?"

    _____

11. _____

12. _____

About My Mommy

My mommy's name is _____.

She has _____ eyes and _____ hair.

Her favorite food is _____.

She does not like to eat _____.

When she was little, she liked to _____

and _____.

Now, she likes to _____

and _____.

_____ makes her happy.

My mommy is sad when _____.

I wish my mommy would _____.

I love my mommy because _____.

Record the child's answers in the blanks. Let the child draw a picture below.

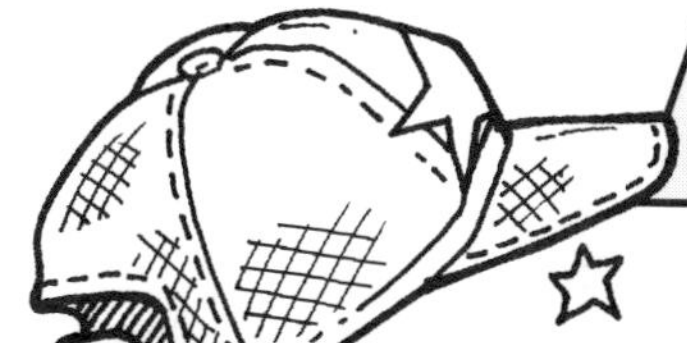

About My Daddy

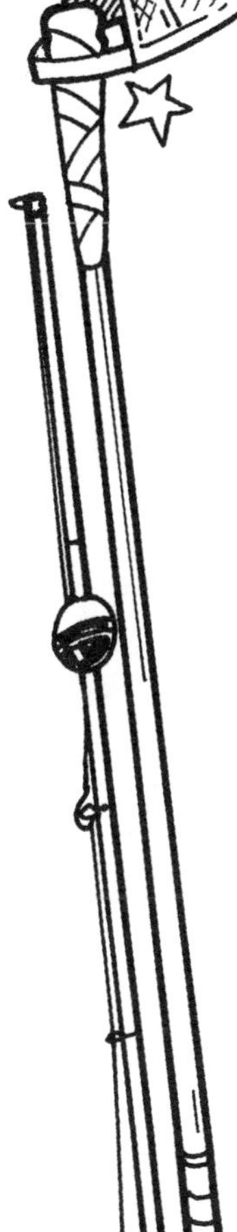

My daddy's name is _____ .

He has _____ eyes and _____ hair.

His favorite food is _____ .

He does not like to eat _____ .

When he was little, he liked to _____

and _____ .

Now, he likes to _____

and _____ .

_____ makes him happy.

My daddy is sad when _____ .

I wish my daddy would _____ .

I love my daddy because _____ .

81

Planner *for* Substitute

Teacher's Name:

Room Number:

Class Roster Attached:

Student with Allergies: **Allergies:**

Student with Allergies: **Allergies:**

Student with Allergies: **Allergies:**

Allergy Action Plan(s) Attached: **Daily Class Schedule Attached:**

Current Classroom Theme:

Special Notes for Circle Time:

Lessons for the Day (Additional notes on the back of this sheet)

Art: Blocks:

Science: Dramatic Play:

Manipulatives: Sand/Water:

Music: Playground:

Story Time:

Special Activities/Guest(s)—*Time, Place & Activity*:

Notes & Insider Information:

Thank you for being our sub!

Sign-Up Sheet for **Parent-Teacher Conferences**

Class:	Teachers:

Parents, please sign up below for a date and time to have a conference about your child. Conferences should last for about _____ minutes.

Thank you!

Date: _____

Time: _____ Student/Family: _____

Time: _____ Student/Family: _____

Time: _____ Student/Family: _____

Time: _____ Student/Family: _____

Time: _____ Student/Family: _____

Time: _____ Student/Family: _____

Time: _____ Student/Family: _____

Time: _____ Student/Family: _____

Time: _____ Student/Family: _____

Date: _____

Time: _____ Student/Family: _____

Time: _____ Student/Family: _____

Time: _____ Student/Family: _____

Time: _____ Student/Family: _____

Time: _____ Student/Family: _____

Time: _____ Student/Family: _____

Time: _____ Student/Family: _____

Time: _____ Student/Family: _____

Time: _____ Student/Family: _____

FORMS FOR TEACHERS TO DISTRIBUTE TO PARENTS

As much as you want to share your students' triumphs with their parents, it's almost impossible to have a meaningful conversation in the drop-off line. The forms in this chapter will help you communicate efficiently with parents.

The chapter begins with the **Orientation for Child and Parents** letter (page 86), which you can personalize and send to parents as soon as you find out which students will be in your classroom. Next, get permission for any event, including field trips, religious and holiday observations, or school programs, by customizing and distributing the **Participation Form** (page 87). Make a big deal about classroom happenings by sending home the **Classroom News** (page 88) or the **What I Did This Week!** form (page 89) on a weekly basis. (An example of a completed form is shown on page 85.) You may also be interested in using one of the newsletter headers (page 57) to personalize and decorate your own formatted newsletters.

● **GOOD IDEA!** ●

For the bathroom section of the **What I Did This Week!** form, complete each day's column if appropriate by writing the time and whether the child was wet or had a bowel movement.

Alert a parent to a minor accident or injury with the **Oops, I Got Hurt!** form (page 90), or let parents know to watch their child for possible illness with the **Your Child Seems Under the Weather** form (page 91).

Other forms in this section include the **Sign-Up Sheet for Class Parties** (pages 92 and 93)—one form highlights secular and Christian holidays and one features Jewish holidays.

● **GOOD IDEA!** ●

Simply white out holidays from either form that you will not celebrate in class before copying it. Post this form in your classroom while parents are coming in for orientation and let them sign up as they wish.

The following communication forms address very specific circumstances and may be time-savers for you. If you customarily ask parents for classroom or project supplies, consider using the **We Need Some Things for Our Classroom!** form (page 94) to request those items. If you have asked a child to bring in something and need to remind the child's parents, send the **Oops, I Forgot . . .** form (page 95). There are also a general **Reminder** form (page 96) and a **Sign & Return** form (page 96) that you can attach to permission slips or progress reports. Program the **We're Going on a Field Trip** form (page 97) and then utilize it to secure permission and chaperones at the same time. If you have parents who habitually pick up their children late, you can first send home the **Late Pickup Notice** (page 98) to warn parents to be on time. Then, if necessary, send the **Late Pickup Charge Notice** (page 98) to invoice them for your time.

There are many other situations when you may wish to send a brief message to a parent. Use the reproducible **Parent Communication Notes** (pages 99–101) for sharing about a child's achievements, requesting that a parent contact you, suggesting activities for children to do at home, or sending a message of gratitude for an act of kindness.

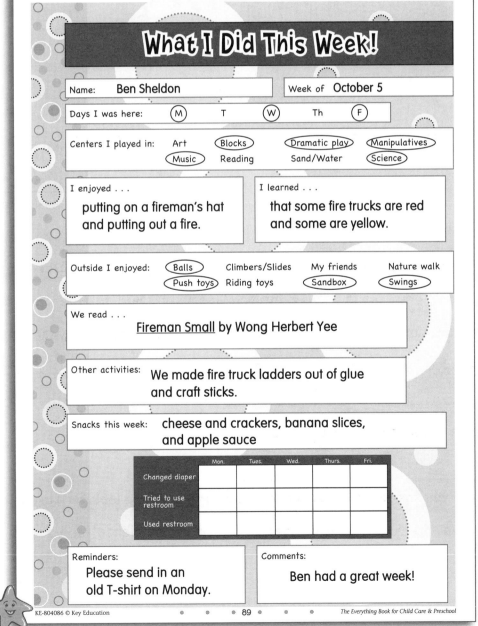

What I Did This Week!

Name: **Ben Sheldon**   Week of **October 5**

Days I was here: (M)   T   (W)   Th   (F)

Centers I played in: Art   (Blocks)   (Dramatic play)   (Manipulatives)   (Music)   Reading   Sand/Water   (Science)

I enjoyed . . .
putting on a fireman's hat and putting out a fire.

I learned . . .
that some fire trucks are red and some are yellow.

Outside I enjoyed: (Balls)   Climbers/Slides   My friends   Nature walk   (Push toys)   Riding toys   (Sandbox)   (Swings)

We read . . .
Fireman Small by Wong Herbert Yee

Other activities: We made fire truck ladders out of glue and craft sticks.

Snacks this week: cheese and crackers, banana slices, and apple sauce

	Mon.	Tues.	Wed.	Thurs.	Fri.
Changed diaper					
Tried to use restroom					
Used restroom					

Reminders:
Please send in an old T-shirt on Monday.

Comments:
Ben had a great week!

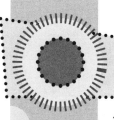

Orientation *for* **Child and Parents**

Dear Parents,

The beginning of the school year is fast approaching. The first day of school is _____. Teachers and staff have been busy making plans and preparing their classrooms. Your child is enrolled in the _____ class. The classroom number is _____.

Your child's teachers are:

_____ and _____.

_____ _____
Phone number   Phone number

_____ _____
E-mail   E-mail

Before school starts, we will have an orientation period for students, parents, and teachers. This is a time for you and your child to meet the teachers, visit the classroom, and ask questions about the upcoming year. Your child's scheduled orientation time is on _____ from _____ to _____. If you need to reschedule this time, please contact your child's teacher.

Thank you for sending your child to our program. We look forward to working with you to make this a wonderful learning experience for your child!

Sincerely,

Participation Form

Class:_____

Teacher:_____ Date: _____

I, _____ , give / do not give my permission
              Parent's name   *Circle one*

for my child to participate in _____ .
                                     Event or celebration

_____   _____
       Parent's signature   *Date*

Participation Form

Class:_____

Teacher:_____ Date: _____

I, _____ , give / do not give my permission
              Parent's name   *Circle one*

for my child to participate in _____ .
                                     Event or celebration

_____   _____
       Parent's signature   *Date*

Classroom News

Teachers:

Date:

What We Did This Week

And, we had fun, too!

Next Week, We Will . . .

Upcoming Events

Happy Birthday to . . .

Reminders

What I Did This Week!

Name: _____   Week of _____

Days I was here: M   T   W   Th   F

Centers I played in: Art   Blocks   Dramatic play   Manipulatives
                         Music   Reading   Sand/Water   Science

I enjoyed . . .

I learned . . .

Outside I enjoyed: Balls   Climbers/Slides   My friends   Nature walk
                       Push toys   Riding toys   Sandbox   Swings

We read . . .

Other activities:

Snacks this week:

	Mon.	Tues.	Wed.	Thurs.	Fri.
Changed diaper					
Tried to use restroom					
Used restroom					

Reminders:

Comments:

Oops, I Got Hurt!

_____ got hurt today.
Child's name

This is what happened: _____

_____

_____

And, here's what we did about it: _____

_____

_____

Teacher: _____

Date: _____

Oops, I Got Hurt!

_____ got hurt today.
Child's name

This is what happened: _____

_____

_____

And, here's what we did about it: _____

_____

_____

Teacher: _____

Date: _____

Your Child Seems Under the Weather

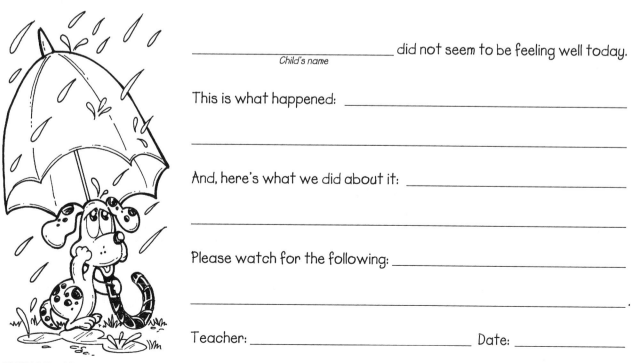

_____ did not seem to be feeling well today.
Child's name

This is what happened: _____

_____

And, here's what we did about it: _____

_____

Please watch for the following: _____

_____ .

Teacher: _____ Date: _____

Your Child Seems Under the Weather

_____ did not seem to be feeling well today.
Child's name

This is what happened: _____

_____

And, here's what we did about it: _____

_____

Please watch for the following: _____

_____ .

Teacher: _____ Date: _____

Sign-Up Sheet : *for* Class Parties

Class: | Teachers:

Parents,

Please sign up for a class party. We would like to have _____ parents per party.

For each party, we will need _____

_____

_____

Thank you!

Fall Festival/Halloween:_____

Thanksgiving: _____

Christmas:_____

New Year's:_____

Valentine's Day: _____

St. Patrick's Day:_____

Easter:_____

End of the Year:_____

Other: _____

Other: _____

Other: _____

Other: _____

Sign-Up Sheet for Class Parties/Events

Class: _____

Teachers: _____

Parents,

Please sign up for a class party or special event. We would like to have _____ parents per party. For each party, we will need _____

_____

_____

Thank you!

· ·

Rosh Hashanah: _____

Yom Kippur: _____

Sukkot: _____

Fall Festival: _____

Thanksgiving: _____

Hanukkah: _____

Valentine's Day: _____

Purim: _____

Passover: _____

Shavuot: _____

End of the Year: _____

Other: _____

I would be willing to help with a Shabbat celebration: _____

_____

_____

We Need Some Things for Our Classroom!

Dear Parents,

We need some help with supplies for upcoming projects. Please save the following household items and have your child bring them to us.

_____

_____

_____

_____

Thank you!

We Need Some Things for Our Classroom!

Dear Parents,

We need some help with supplies for upcoming projects. Please save the following household items and have your child bring them to us.

_____

_____

_____

_____

Thank you!

Reminder

This is to remind you to _____

_____ on or by _____.

Thank you!

Sign & Return

Please sign this paper and return it with your child. Thanks!

Sign & Return

Please sign this paper and return it with your child. Thanks!

We're Going on a Field Trip

Please complete the form below and return it to school.

My child _____ has permission to go to
                    Child's name

_____ on _____ with the class. I am / am not
     Location   *Date*   *Circle one*

able to serve as a chaperone.

_____   _____
     Parent's signature   *Date*

- -

We're Going on a Field Trip

Please complete the form below and return it to school.

My child _____ has permission to go to
                    Child's name

_____ on _____ with the class. I am / am not
     Location   *Date*   *Circle one*

able to serve as a chaperone.

_____   _____
     Parent's signature   *Date*

Late Pickup Notice

Dear _____,

You were late picking up your child on _____.

Please remember that our pickup time is _____.

Thank you!

Your school logo here

Late Pickup Charge Notice

Dear _____,

You were late _____ picking up your child on

_____. We will have to charge you _____

for the extra school time.

Sincerely,

Guess What I did?

_____

_____

_____

Ask me about . . .

_____

_____

_____

Today I learned . . .

_____

_____

_____

Hooray for me!

_____
_____
_____

We are excited about . . .

_____
_____
_____

Please contact me.
We need to discuss . . .

Call me   E-mail me

Fun-to-Do Activity!

Dear Parents,

We are _____ in class.

Here is a great activity you can do with your child at home! _____

_____

_____

Thank you!

Book Boredom Buster!

Dear Parents,

We are reading _____ .

Here is a great activity you can do with your child at home! _____

_____

_____

Thank you!

INVITATIONS AND DECORATIVE BORDERS

Invitations and decorative borders can be used at any time of the year. The borders in this book will help school-to-parent correspondence look cohesive and professional, yet still lighthearted enough for a preschool. Invitations are programmable to make them flexible. You may personalize reduced copies of invitations with your facility's or school's letterhead.

The **You're Invited!** and **Please Come to Our Parent Meeting** forms (page 103) are suitable for inviting parents to any event. Use **The Week of the Young Child Event Calendar** and **Invitation** (page 104) during the weeklong celebration of preschool-aged children if your school holds events for parents, such as classroom read alongs, performances, socials, and playdates. Parents will also enjoy attending **Come Meet My Friends** (page 105), a great event to host a few weeks into the school year that will help them get acquainted with the classmates their children have been talking about at home. The left side of this page is an invitation to a social event, and the right side is a programmable class list for parents to keep at home.

Treat parents with **Doughnuts with Daddies** and **Muffins with Mommies** (page 106) events. Instead of having to rush through drop off, parents will enjoy spending a few minutes at school eating breakfast snacks and socializing with other families. Parents will appreciate not having to fix breakfast as well. It is a good idea to host these two days separately to spread out parent involvement.

To welcome new parents to school before the rush of orientation, invite them to enjoy coffee

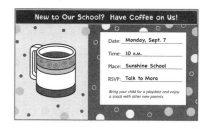

and refreshments while their children play on the school playground. Send home the **New to Our School? Have Coffee on Us!** invitation (page 107) and host this meeting a week or so before school starts, if possible, so that most families have finished their summer vacations, and their children will remember friendly faces from the gathering. If your school or facility prefers a more formal social event, plan an evening get-together with built-in babysitting at the school so that parents are free to meet and greet you, the staff, and each other without childcare responsibilities. Send home the **A Night Out on Us!** invitation (page 107) with more "grown-up" art to signify the relative formality of the parents-only event.

Use the **Seasonal and Theme-Related Borders** (pages 108–128) throughout the school year as appropriate. The borders are especially useful for supply lists, holiday-event notices, class-party reminders, class newsletters, and other happenings. Your students may also be interested in using the full-page or half-page borders to create invitations.

You're Invited!

To _____

Date _____ **Time** _____

Place _____

RSVP _____

Please Come to Our Parent Meeting

Date: _____

Time: _____

Place: _____

Topic: _____

_____

RSVP: _____

The Week of the Young Child
Event Calendar

Date:

Monday	Tuesday	Wednesday	Thursday	Friday

The Week of the Young Child

Please join us for _____ .

Date: _____

Time: _____

Place: _____

RSVP: _____

Look Who Is in My Class

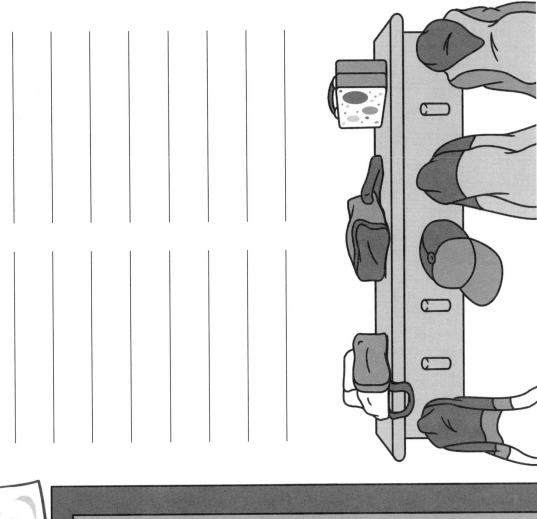

_____

_____

_____

_____

_____

Come Meet My Friends

in _____'s Class

Date: _____

Time: _____

Place: _____

RSVP: _____

Doughnuts with Daddies

Daddies, please join us for a light breakfast
with your children.

Date: _____

Time: _____

Place: _____

RSVP: _____

Muffins with Mommies

Mommies, please join us for a light breakfast
with your children.

Date: _____

Time: _____

Place: _____

RSVP: _____

New to Our School? Have Coffee on Us!

Date: _____

Time: _____

Place: _____

RSVP: _____

Bring your child for a playdate and enjoy a snack with other new parents.

A Night Out on Us!

Date: _____

Time: _____

Place: _____

RSVP: _____

Come visit the classroom! Child care will be provided.

112

115

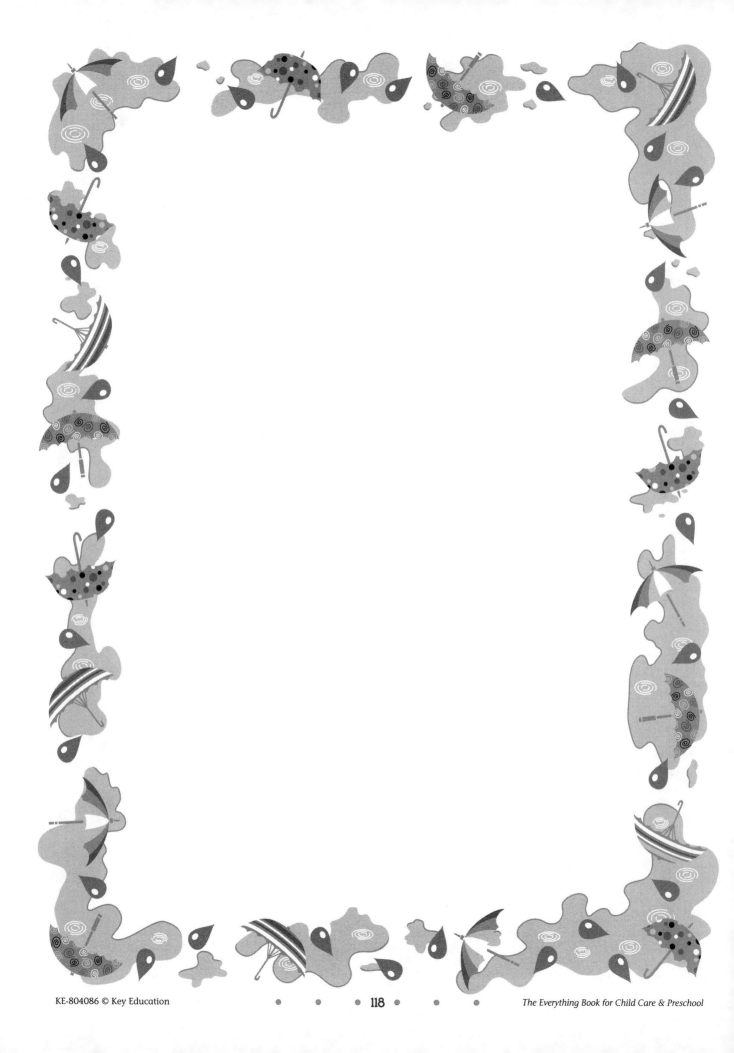

119

120

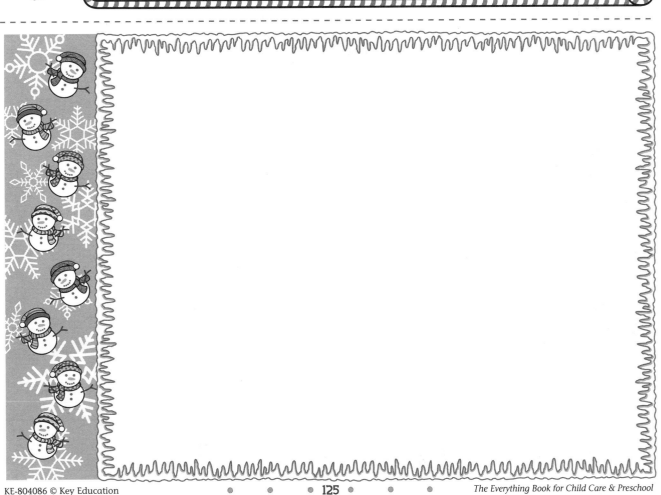

128

NEWSLETTERS FOR PARENTS

The same subjects come up over and over in preschool. Often, it is easier to give parents some reading material so that they have background information on an issue or learning trend before you talk with them about their child. Here are a few newsletters you can use to keep parents in the loop about typical growth patterns, common issues, learning styles, and other subjects of interest. Also included are lists of fun books for each age group and ideas for creative play around the house.

The **Developmental Milestones** newsletters (pages 130–135) briefly explain the typical developmental stages and milestones for each age from infancy to five. Each letter includes information about how children develop at different rates. You will also find suggestions for parents on **Building Fine Motor** and **Gross Motor Skills** (pages 136 and 137).

The **Raising Children Who Love to Learn** newsletters are for parents who want to focus on their children's learning at home. Share these newsletters to encourage learning through play and fun activities. Topics include **How Is Your Child Smart?** (explaining multiple intelligences on page 138), **Raising a Reader** (page 139), **Raising a Mathematician** (page 140), **Raising a Scientist** (page 141), **Raising an Engineer** (page 142), **Raising an Artist** (page 143), and **Raising a Child Who Loves Music** (page 144). More general newsletters include **Learning Through Play** (page 145), **Great Around-the-House Toys** (page 146), and a list of titles of **Special Books** selected for children of each age from infancy through five (pages 147–152).

The final group of newsletters deals with all kinds of issues that can sometimes be challenging to talk about with parents. These are good to send home to alert parents to potential dangers or to help educate them about typical behaviors that occur with preschoolers. Topics include **What to Do if Your Child Is Biting** (page 153), **What to Do if Your Child Doesn't Want to Go to School** (page 154), **Teaching Your Child to Be a Kind Friend** (page 155), **Bullying** (page 156), **Stranger Danger** (page 157), **The Importance of Eating Healthful Foods** (page 158), **Keeping Your Child Active** (page 159), and **Potty Time!** (page 160).

Developmental Milestones *for* **Infants**

Milestones are common skills and abilities that pediatricians use to guide them as they evaluate a child's growth and development. All children are different and will achieve these milestones at different times. So, as you watch your child acquire these skills, also remember to enjoy your child as a unique individual.

By three months, your child can probably:

* lift his head and shoulders while on tummy*
* respond to sounds by turning her head
* gurgle and coo
* follow objects with his eyes
* smile and laugh
* recognize mom's and dad's faces and scents
* bear weight on her legs
  (Because it is recommended that infants sleep on their backs, this skill may come later.)

By six months, your child can probably:

* hold up his head steadily
* turn over (eventually in both directions)
* grab (and possibly release) objects
* play with her own hands and feet
* coo and babble in response to your talk
* reach for objects and "mouth" them
* sit without support

By nine months, your child can probably:

* babble and may repeat syllables ("ma-ma-ma")
* pass an object from one hand to the other
* sweep his hand to pick up an object
* point
* wave good-bye
* grasp objects between thumb and pointer finger
* crawl
* stand with support
* bang objects to make sounds (cause and effect)

By 12 months, your child can probably:

* make sounds that are like words (may say words to name objects and people)
* explore while "cruising" (walking while holding on to furniture)
* understand "no"
* put objects in a container and pour them out
* play infant games (peekaboo, "Itsy Bitsy Spider," etc.)
* drink from a sippy cup
* stand alone or take a few steps (between 12 and 15 months)
* understand and follow simple instructions

Developmental Milestones *for* **Toddlers**
(Ages 12–24 Months)

Milestones are common skills and abilities that pediatricians use to guide them as they evaluate a child's growth and development. All children are different and will achieve these milestones at different times. So, as you watch your child acquire these skills, also remember to enjoy your child as a unique individual.

By 15 months, your child can probably:

* use phrases of two words or more ("No, Mama!")
* respond to instructions ("Give me a kiss!")
* say "No!" often and emphatically
* walk well
* hold out his arms or legs to "help" get dressed
* roll a ball back and forth to someone
* push or pull a toy while walking
* use a spoon or fork to feed herself
* scribble with a crayon or pencil

By 18 months, your child can probably:

* use six or more words
* express food preferences
* throw a tantrum when frustrated
* use objects like a phone, broom, or doll for dramatic play
* climb
* dance
* stack three or more blocks

By 21 months, your child can probably:

* understand the meanings of at least 200 words
* point and name objects
* throw a ball overhand
* walk up and down stairs
* run
* remove clothing
* stack at least six blocks

By 24 months, your child can probably:

* use at least 70 words
* follow directions with two steps ("Take off your hat and bring it to Daddy.")
* talk about herself ("Molly likes crackers.")
* ask, "Why?"
* sort and categorize items
* name at least six body parts
* point out gender differences
* sing songs
* kick a ball
* jump

Developmental Milestones *for* **Two-Year-Olds**
(Ages 25–36 Months)

Milestones are common skills and abilities that pediatricians use to guide them as they evaluate a child's growth and development. All children are different and will achieve these milestones at different times. So, as you watch your child acquire these skills, also remember to enjoy your child as a unique individual.

By 30 months, your child can probably:
* speak clearly most of the time
* use pronouns correctly, especially "I"
* recognize some letters and colors
* play with friends
* use adjectives
* balance on one foot
* wash and dry his hands
* brush her teeth with help
* draw a circle

By 36 months, your child can probably:
* recognize letters and numbers
* talk about how to use an object ("The airplane flies in the air.")
* follow three-step instructions ("Finish snack, get your trash, and throw it away.")
* demonstrate understanding of position words (*on, under, inside*)
* show feelings on command (happy, sad, silly)
* balance on either foot
* use the potty in the daytime
* pull up pants with an elastic waistband
* brush his own hair and teeth

Developmental Milestones *for* **Three-Year-Olds**

Milestones are common skills and abilities that pediatricians use to guide them as they evaluate a child's growth and development. All children are different and will achieve these milestones at different times. So, as you watch your child acquire these skills, also remember to enjoy your child as a unique individual.

During the third year, your child will probably learn to:

❖ recognize complicated cause-and-effect relationships ("If I take his toy, he will be sad.")

❖ speak in sentences of at least three to five words

❖ point out colors and numbers in conversation

❖ ask for help

❖ prefer to play near other children

❖ take turns

❖ make simple choices ("I want to play with dolls, not blocks.")

❖ recognize others' moods

❖ follow consistent routines

❖ manage transitions when given fair warning

❖ seek independence

❖ rely on hands-on experiences and the five senses to stimulate learning

❖ make herself clearly understood nearly all of the time

❖ throw and catch large balls

❖ climb ladders

❖ pedal

❖ alternate feet going up and down stairs

❖ walk on a balance bar

❖ paint using a pencil grip (rather than gripping the brush with a fist)

❖ put together simple jigsaw puzzles

❖ cut with scissors

❖ manipulate play dough well

Developmental Milestones *for* **Four-Year-Olds**

Milestones are common skills and abilities that pediatricians use to guide them as they evaluate a child's growth and development. All children are different and will achieve these milestones at different times. So, as you watch your child acquire these skills, also remember to enjoy your child as a unique individual.

During the fourth year, your child will probably learn to:

❖ use complex sentences ("Daddy closed the door so that the dog would stay inside.")

❖ use and understand over 1,000 words

❖ solve problems using reason and logic

❖ embrace new activities, games, and situations quickly, as long as she has adequate preparation and knows what to expect

❖ connect pictures with words in environmental print

❖ understand passage of time, but may not grasp the duration of time (For example, a child will know that yesterday was in the past but may not understand how long ago yesterday actually was.)

❖ use words rather than actions to express emotion

❖ lie

❖ play cooperatively

❖ gallop, skip, tiptoe, and balance very well

❖ make sharp turns or sudden stops while running

❖ catch a bounced ball

❖ complete most grooming tasks independently

❖ print some letters and draw shapes

❖ cut on a straight line

❖ use a spoon and fork with ease

Developmental Milestones *for* Five-Year-Olds

Milestones are common skills and abilities that pediatricians use to guide them as they evaluate a child's growth and development. All children are different and will achieve these milestones at different times. So, as you watch your child acquire these skills, also remember to enjoy your child as a unique individual.

During the fifth year, your child will probably learn to:

❖ use plurals, tenses, and all parts of speech correctly
❖ recognize her name in print
❖ understand opposites
❖ learn simple addition and subtraction using objects ("I have three oranges and two apples. How many pieces of fruit do I have altogether?")
❖ talk in front of the whole class
❖ tell the difference between right and wrong/honesty and dishonesty
❖ seek out and value friends
❖ conform to a group in order to fit in
❖ play elaborate make-believe
❖ skate
❖ jump rope
❖ hold a pencil like an adult
❖ color within the lines of a picture
❖ draw a stick person
❖ lace and try to tie shoes
❖ cut out pictures and shapes
❖ string beads on a lace

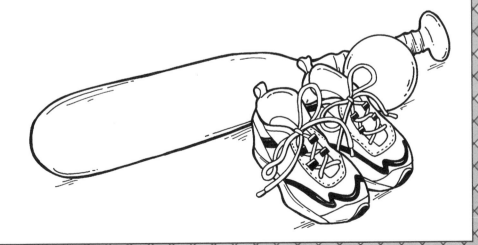

Building Fine Motor Skills

Building skills that involve moving and controlling the hand muscles is extremely important for young children's independence. Children cannot feed themselves unless they can hold spoons and forks correctly. They cannot become fully potty trained until they can unbutton their pants. They need good fine motor skills to write. Here are some ways to help foster fine motor skills.

Infants: Grasping is the first fine motor skill children acquire. Put inviting objects within your baby's reach to encourage grasping. Give your baby blocks, fabric toys, and even rattles to squeeze and manipulate. Hold some objects over her head so that she has to reach for them. Watch as she progresses from grasping with her entire hand to a pincer grasp—grasping between her thumb and pointer finger—and from just grasping to dropping and transferring objects. DO NOT give your child any small object that could present a choking hazard.

Toddlers: Use your toddler's growing independence to improve fine motor skills. Teach him to pull up his own pants and turn doorknobs. Let him "write" with crayons while you pay bills, handle nontoxic play dough, stack blocks, and place rings on a peg. Toddlers love to dump objects, so give him opportunities to dump out blocks, wooden puzzles, or socks. Have him replace the objects before he dumps them out again for extra fine-motor practice. Once your child is sitting well, you can also provide bathtub toys. Trying to hold on to slippery, soapy objects makes for a giggly bath time!

Two-year-olds: Children continue to benefit from working on fine motor tasks that use both hands. Celebrate your two-year-old's fine motor skills by letting her unwrap gifts! The fun of ripping paper is as exciting as the gift inside. Your two-year-old can also learn how to unbutton and unsnap her own clothes, open a jar, use a tiny broom and dustpan to sweep, and transfer cotton swabs from one container to another using a pincer grip. Two-year-olds are also ready for safety scissors with supervision. And, don't miss any opportunity to let her push a doorbell or elevator button!

Three- to Four-Year-Olds: Scissor skills are even more important for this age, as are skills that involve getting ready to write. Offer your child opportunities to trace and cut out shapes, letters, and pictures. Depending on your child's number recognition skills, make dot-to-dot puzzles and mazes available for him to complete. Correct your child's pencil grip as necessary, focusing on the tripod grip (between thumb and two fingers). Provide tools such as plastic tweezers or tongs to move cotton balls or other small objects. Continue to build with blocks, but add more complex building materials, such as beads and laces, large magnetic building sets, and blocks that link together. Three- to four-year-olds are also ready for more complex puzzles.

Four- to Five-Year-Olds: Children at this age need more practice with the same skills, but you can add new ones, as well. Help your child learn to do lacing cards, zip clothing, tie shoes, and continue to copy shapes, lines, and even numbers and letters on paper. Also, continue helping your child use the correct pencil grip. If you have a large, sturdy computer keyboard, let her practice pushing individual keys.

Building Gross Motor Skills

Gross motor activities build the coordination and strength of large muscle groups. It is very important for children to accomplish growth in gross motor development during their preschool years. Even though their explorations sometimes make parents' palms a little sweaty, this is the age when children should fine-tune skills like walking, running, skipping, hopping, crawling, climbing, galloping, and swinging on swings.

Some children will naturally be drawn to gross motor activities, while others prefer quiet, fine motor activities. It is important to have a balance; both skill sets are important. Encourage gross motor development by offering lots of movement activities that use large muscle groups. Here are some ideas to get your child moving!

First and most obvious—go outside! Children are naturally encouraged to make bigger movements while in open spaces. Take your child to a big field and watch how she runs, jumps, and plays while trying to "conquer" all that space.

If you have a good open area and the materials, create an obstacle course for your child to maneuver through. Use hoops on the ground (or draw large circles on pavement with chalk) for him to jump in and out of, place a balance beam (a flat board) on the ground for him to walk across, and add a rope for your child to swing on or a low obstacle he must jump over. Changing the course frequently will challenge his brain as well as his muscle groups.

If it is rainy or you are otherwise stuck inside, you can still create some gross motor activities for your child. Create an obstacle course from pillows. "Fluff" a sheet in the air and let your child run under it and squat before the sheet floats down around her. Or, have a dance party. Dance around the room to music and when the music stops, instruct your child to freeze! Have her use a different movement when the music starts again, such as walking, hopping, tiptoeing, etc. Change the music so that she has to adapt to different rhythms.

Finally, use simple, everyday tasks to encourage gross motor skill development. If your child is over 18 months old, help him practice climbing stairs using alternating feet. Teach your child to pump his own legs while swinging, close his own car door, balance on one foot when he has to wait with you in line at the grocery store, and carry a bag of groceries from the car to the house. (Simple acts of carrying and walking improve the muscles that control balance while adding strength, as well.) At home, let your child help you sweep, dust, vacuum, wash low windows, and put away his own toys and clothing. Pedaling is an important skill, so make sure he has access to a riding toy either at home or at preschool. Children have plenty of energy and need many outlets for it. The energy is what drives their development. So get moving!

How Is Your Child Smart?

Every child is smart in some way. The term multiple intelligences was originated by Dr. Howard Gardner, professor of education at Harvard University. The theory asserts that most people possess more than one type of intelligence. Gardner identified eight types of intelligences: linguistic ("word smart"), logical-mathematical ("logic smart"), spatial ("picture smart"), bodily-kinesthetic ("body smart"), musical ("music smart"), interpersonal ("people smart"), intrapersonal ("self smart"), and naturalistic ("nature smart").

Schools that apply Gardner's theory to their teaching methods seek out ways to reach children through the different intelligences. For example, if a teacher wants to teach children about space while addressing each intelligence, she could have them do some of the following lessons:

1. Word Smart: Read books about space and learn the names of the planets.
2. Logic Smart: Countdown to blastoff, count the planets, or have children learn how much they would weigh on the moon.
3. Picture Smart: Draw and color pictures or make models of each planet.
4. Body Smart: Act out spinning on an axis while rotating around a child who is pretending to be the sun.
5. Music Smart: Play music from popular films about space and discuss why the music sounds "spacelike."
6. People Smart: Let children work together to pretend to be a crew of astronauts flying to the moon.
7. Self Smart: Ask children to name and draw their favorite planets and explain their choices.
8. Nature Smart: Go outside and observe the moon during the daytime.

To help your child become more aware of his different learning strengths, try to apply similar types of lessons when your child is interested in a new hobby. Perhaps the best way to encourage growth and development in all areas of intelligence is to watch your child play. What does he gravitate toward? Does he love to be outside? Does he always want to draw and color? Does he like to play pretend with groups of other children, or does he prefer to play alone? When he plays, does he push himself physically and seem very coordinated? Does he want to hear music while he plays? Does he always want to pick out a new book at the library and tell you about it after he reads it? Does he like to count his crackers as he eats them?

Whatever your child likes, doing more of it will help her learn other skills. As you engage your child in play at home, try to offer different experiences that will both enhance what she is good at and sharpen and expand skills in other areas. A well-rounded child is far more likely to find ways to learn and persevere in both school and life.

Raising a Reader

Reading is one of the most important skills for a child to acquire. It is the key to almost everything else your child will do in school—and to many things done outside of school as well. Follow these suggestions to raise a child who delights in reading.

- Treat book time as if it is one of the best parts of your day. If possible, avoid sending a rowdy child to her room to read books; reading should not feel like a punishment.

- Use blocks, wooden letters, paper letters, or magnetic letters to help your child touch and see letters as he learns them.

- Try to spend at least 20 minutes reading to your child each day.

- Get on your child's level to see what print he can see. Point out words everywhere you go. You will be surprised how quickly your child will learn to read words on labels of favorite foods, on the logos of favorite restaurants, and on his clothing.

- Chances are, your child will pick a favorite book and want you to read it over and over until you never want to see it again. Bear with her. Ask her to read the book to you. You may be surprised to find that she can recite it back to you easily and may even recognize some of the words on her own.

- Road signs are a great way to help your child spot familiar words because they come with bold print, interesting shapes, and bright colors.

- Let your child see you reading and writing as often as possible. Whether you are reading junk mail, a novel, the comics, or e-mail, help her see that reading is a treat and something that "big people do."

- Give your child opportunities to create his own reading material by "writing" on a piece of paper. Even if you cannot read it at all, ask him to tell you what his writing says, just as you would if he had drawn a picture. Or, let him draw several pieces of art and tell you a story around them. Write the story at the bottoms of the pages; then, staple them together to make a book you can reread.

- When your child starts to recognize words, write words naming household objects on index cards and attach them to the objects themselves. After your child recognizes the words, mix them up and let him put them back on their correct objects.

- As your child learns to read, record or videotape her reading and play it back to her. She will be amazed to see herself as a real reader.

Raising a Mathematician

Some children seem to gravitate toward numbers. Perhaps your child looks for numbers on school buses, sorts or counts cars or farm animals, or asks you to solve math problems. Encourage your child's love of math with these activities.

- Start by counting the things your child knows best—her body parts! In the mirror, count her eyes, her ears, etc.

- Children can learn numbers in the same way they learn letters. Look for them in books, on food labels, on signs, and at the bottoms of pages.

- Sing as many counting and number songs and chants as you can think of with your child, such as "One, Two, Buckle My Shoe."

- Use snack time to help your child count. Give him a small bowl of a favorite finger food. Tell him to eat three pieces, then two pieces, and so on, helping him count out each portion. Eventually, you can ask him to count out separate amounts, and then count the total to tell you how many he will eat altogether.

- Encourage counting by using a behavior chart and colorful star stickers as a math tool. Help your child choose a goal, such as using the potty seven times. Promise a small reward when your child earns seven stars, such as a new book from the library. Each time your child uses the potty, help her put a star on the chart; then, count the total number of stars together.

- If you have a child that needs to move to learn, use movement to inspire counting. Have her dribble a ball once or throw three balls or jump six times. Help her count out the movements as she performs them.

- On the way to preschool, have a number scavenger hunt. Assign your child a numeral and have him look for that numeral on houses, license plates, street signs, exit signs, and speed limit signs. (Five is a good number to begin with because many speed limits end with five.)

- Recognizing and working with shapes and geometry is an early, accessible math skill. Help your child sort objects by shape. For example, provide a bowl of different cereal pieces (without any added coloring) and ask him to sort the cereals by shape. Next, start a pattern, such as circle, square, circle, square, and ask him to continue it.

- Use a child's favorite activity to encourage sorting. Provide guidance as needed. Otherwise, you might not recognize your child's sorting criteria. If your child loves dolls, ask her to put all of her grown-up dolls in one chair and the babies in another chair.

Raising a Scientist

Science comes naturally to many children because they are naturally inquisitive. Here's how to make the most of that curiosity.

- The whole world is a science experiment to infants and toddlers. They are constantly batting at objects, mouthing them, and then climbing them or throwing them to see what will happen. Provide as many safe opportunities for exploration as you can to encourage your child's natural curiosity.

- Follow-through is important because it teaches your child that he can find out answers to almost any question. When a child asks, "Why?" over and over, take the time to help him find out the answers. For example, if a child asks how fireflies glow in the dark, look up the answer (their bodies make chemicals that glow) and explain why it happens (probably to help them find other fireflies). Then, head outside at dusk to observe some fireflies.

- Adjust your answers to your child's level. A child may not understand the word *bioluminescence*, but she may understand the firefly answer given above. Use words she can understand to explain concepts.

- Simple experiments sharpen children's senses and encourage them to be inquisitive. Examine everyday objects and events in a scientific way. Let her examine dryer lint and talk about why lint collects in the lint trap. Let your child examine a variety of objects, such as a bar of soap, table tennis balls, a large pebble, and a toy boat, and predict which objects will sink and which will float. Then, invite her to drop the objects into a pan of water. Let her tell whether an egg has been cooked by spinning a raw egg and a hardboiled egg on a tabletop to discover which one does not spin very well. Let your child add food coloring to water and then mix the different colors of water to see what new colors result or find out what happens when she scatters pepper in a dish of water and then squeezes a drop of soap into the dish.

- Take your child on nature walks in your backyard or neighborhood park. There is so much to discover in the fascinating world of flowers, leaves, rocks, bugs, birds, tadpoles, and so on. Let him describe what he observes, such as what colors are seen, how something feels (textures), how various objects compare in size, or how certain animals move.

- Follow your child's lead. If your child is fascinated by dogs, look at pictures of dogs and talk about their body parts, their sizes and colors, and that some dogs learn to do tricks. Visit a pet shop or a friend that has different types of dogs. If your child loves machinery, talk about the different jobs machines do and watch machines at a construction site.

Raising an Engineer

Some children seem to crave the experience of taking things apart and then putting them back together again. These are the children who want to know how things work. Use some of these ideas to satisfy your young tinkerer.

- Explain to your child how things work. For example, demonstrate exactly how your window blinds move up and down. Show your child which levers on the car's steering column control the wipers and the turn signal. Or, have her watch for the traffic lights as they turn.

- Take field trips to practical places. A child who loves to build will enjoy a scheduled visit to a factory, a racetrack (bring earplugs!), or a restored historic village where people do things with their hands.

- This is the child who will help around the house! Let him use a small vacuum, hand you tools while you install new cabinet hardware, or help you plan out and dig a new garden.

- Provide opportunities for tinkering with screws and screwdrivers, hammers, pliers, measuring tape, and levels. (Make sure your child is supervised and is old enough not to mouth small objects before doing this activity.)

- Point out simple machines (lever, inclined plane, wedge, pulley, screw, and wheel and axle) to your child whenever you see them. For example, pushing a stroller or shopping cart up a ramp uses both a plane and a wheel and axle. Work with your child until he is able to recognize these machines when he sees them.

- When purchasing toys for your child, choose those that have an element of assembly to them. Many games and toys have to be put together before they can be played with, and this extra opportunity to build will be enjoyable and instructive for some children.

- Give your child a chance to have a say-so when rearranging furniture in your house or her bedroom or playroom. Changing the environment keeps spaces interesting for children.

- There are endless building toys available for your child to construct and deconstruct. Combine wooden blocks, snap-together blocks, tape, string, hook-and-loop tape, wooden train tracks, car racetracks, and other building toys on one surface. Encourage your child to combine the toys and materials to make terrific contraptions or busy villages.

Raising an Artist

Some children seem drawn to beautiful objects. If your child doodles, likes to choose and match clothes for school, and loves art materials, use these activities to create rich at-home experiences.

- Let your child gather outdoor objects, such as leaves, nuts, flowers, twigs, feathers, etc. Help him carefully glue the objects to a piece of poster board to make a collage.

- If you have a digital camera and you trust your child not to drop it, take her outside to snap some of her own pictures. Print out the pictures if possible and frame a few for her room.

- Always keep scrap paper and crayons in the car so that your child can draw while he is strapped into his car seat. It helps to attach the paper to a clipboard to provide a hard surface to draw on and to keep paper from going everywhere.

- Help your child recreate some of the art from her favorite books. Try torn paper collages after reading Eric Carle books or black-and-white art after reading *Kitten's First Full Moon* by Kevin Henkes (Greenwillow, 2004). Don't worry if the art is not recognizable; the important part of the experience is using the different media.

- Visit a local art gallery. Ask your child what he sees in each piece of art. You might be surprised at some of the answers!

- Create an old-fashioned art experience for your child. Dress your child in a smock and provide paints, brushes, and water. Then, arrange a still life for her to paint or set up an easel outside in front of an interesting outdoor scene. Let her try to paint what she sees.

- Use art to inspire a compare and contrast discussion. For example, show your child a Dr. Seuss book and a book about animals with realistic photographs. Ask her to tell you the differences between the two books' artwork.

- Purchase some inexpensive wooden letters (the letters in your child's name) and some child-friendly paint at a craft store. Let your child paint the letters in any way he likes. Let the letters dry on a hard surface, such as a ceramic plate (newspaper will stick to the wet paint). Then, attach them to his door with hook-and-loop tape or place them on the door frame over the door to his room.

- Display your child's artwork proudly by creating a simple gallery. Hang a length of string across a wall and attach spring-type clothespins to it. Use the clothespins to hang artwork from the string.

Raising a Child Who Loves Music

Music is often used to teach other skills. For example, many children learn to say their letters using the "Alphabet Song." Here are some ideas to help your child enjoy music for music's sake.

→ Teach your child to hear and pay attention. Listen with him for specific sounds. Can he hear the birds? The crunch of a car's tires on a gravel driveway? The leaves in the trees? Sirens? Music from passing cars?

→ Never miss an opportunity to sing to your child. Lullabies become like favorite stories that can be enjoyed over and over. Even if your choice of a lullaby is unconventional (like "Take Me Out to the Ballgame" or the theme to your favorite TV show), your child will learn to love the melody and associate it with quiet, comforting times.

→ Children love silly songs. Invest in some CDs of children's music you can enjoy and then play the music in your car or late in the afternoon when many children get irritable.

→ Pair music with movement as often as possible. Songs with motions like "The Wheels on the Bus" or a game of freeze (in which you stop the music and everyone freezes), reinforce gross motor skills and music appreciation, as will a fun dance party session with family members.

→ Play a variety of music for your child that goes beyond children's music. Songs from your favorite radio station or those that play oldies, jazz, classical, disco, and even holiday music can all capture your child's imagination. With any radio music, pay attention to the lyrics—children are excellent mimics, and you may be surprised at what songs you hear your child repeating after hearing them just once!

→ You can provide instruments without spending any money. Pots and pans and spoons become drums and drumsticks, plastic containers filled with dried beans become shakers, a cardboard tube becomes a microphone or a horn, and a small broom becomes an air guitar.

→ If you have a local symphony that caters to children, take advantage of their programs. Most are designed to keep little ones entertained. By the age of four, some children may even be ready for concerts.

→ Check out children's musical selections from the library. Make a habit of picking up some new music each time you and your child choose new books.

→ After your child learns to sing a favorite song, record her singing it and play it back often.

→ Try to give your child supervised opportunities to "pet" instruments—handle a violin gently, play a piano or keyboard, or blow into a recorder. Your child may pick up the ability to play music more easily than you think!

Learning Through Play

Children learn best through playing. When children are given free playtime, they learn problem solving, critical thinking, and other important skills. Here are some examples of the skills children learn while playing.

- A dollhouse or toy farm is a great tool for young children. Putting the furniture in the correct rooms or the animals in their pens teaches children how to sort—an important prerequisite for logic and analytic thinking.

- Dump out an inviting selection of blocks or balls in the middle of a group of children. In addition to fine motor skills acquired when stacking the blocks or gross motor skills acquired while throwing and kicking the balls, children will learn how to get along, take turns, and impose their own order on a situation.

- Dress-up clothes encourage children to "try on" different roles. Dolls, action figures, and stuffed animals add to the fun. As children pretend to be teachers, parents, or firefighters, they can also act out (and work through) conflicts and intense emotions like fear or anger.

- Parents are often told to read to their children. Enhance their reading experiences through play. Children's books are a wealth of play ideas. For example, read *The Three Little Pigs* and then act it out with your child. Encourage your child to pretend parts of his favorite books and join in as often as possible.

- Provide access to gross motor toys such as balls, push toys, riding toys, and safe climbing apparatuses with which children can challenge themselves physically.

Make your child's play area accessible and inviting with these ideas:

- Put toys at eye level so that children are invited to play with what they see.

- Change the scenery. Rotate toys in and out of the play area. Arrange familiar toys in new ways so that children see them differently and are encouraged to play with them. For example, on a low table, build a small block village and add cars one week. The next week, replace this scene with dolls and cardboard boxes with which to make houses.

- One of the most inviting ways to encourage your child to play creatively is to play with your child! Get on your child's level and follow her lead in a pretend game of any kind.

- When your child is old enough for playdates (usually between ages three and four), set up a safe area for play, provide enough toys to go around, and let children interact on their own as much as possible so that their play is spontaneous. This becomes easier as children get older.

Newsletter for Parents

Great Around-the-House Toys

One of the best ways to encourage creativity in children is to let them use familiar objects in a not-so-familiar way. Provide access to some of these objects and watch the children use their imaginations. If one object is not a big hit, do not worry—another one is sure to be. (Note: if your child is under age three or is still mouthing objects, do not allow access to anything that could be a choking hazard.)

- Very young children (and some older ones) will enjoy playing with a basket of scrap fabric. Provide pieces that are large enough for your child to closely examine the pattern, texture, weight, and other properties (such as whether the fabric has a nap or whether it wrinkles).

- Cardboard tubes are fabulous found objects. Keep a shopping bag in a closet and drop in clean, dry, paper towel and toilet paper tubes until the bag is full. Provide rubber bands, tape, or self-adhesive hook-and-loop tape so that your child can connect the tubes. Help her create pretend binoculars, build towers, or make tunnels for cars or small animals. Small children can use paper towel tubes as indoor baseball bats with very soft foam balls.

- If you have an older child, let her play with a container of marbles. The colors, round shape, and smooth texture are appealing to most children. Marbles are also great when paired with cardboard tubes (see above).

- Provide an exciting sensory experience with a large, plastic jar filled with plastic bead necklaces. Children can learn their colors, develop fine motor skills by handling the beads, and, of course, wear them for dress up.

- Children love playing with grown-up work tools. If you have a calculator with large buttons that isn't especially delicate, let your child play with it or an old computer keyboard. He will develop fine motor skills from pushing the buttons as well as begin to recognize numbers and letters with your help.

- If you use paper plates and decorative paper napkins, keep a stash of them in a basket for your child. Colorful napkins can become dolls' blankets, pretend quilt squares (join them with tape), or plots in a garden if the napkins happen to be decorated with flowers or vegetables. Paper plates and fancy napkins are also wonderful for impromptu tea parties—and the "tea set" is different every time.

- Measuring cups and spoons are wonderful toys. They usually have sturdy handles and can be used for playing in a sink or bathtub during bath time.

- Do not forget to take advantage of found objects in nature. Any group of similar objects can be used for play. Pinecones, seedpods, unshelled nuts, rocks, shells, and even colorful fall leaves can be collected, examined, compared, sorted, and then put back into nature.

Special Books for Your Infant

It's never too early to start reading to your baby. Babies love hearing the sound of their parents' voices, looking at pictures, and spending time close together while reading. Eventually, your baby will be curious enough to want to hold the book alone and then to mouth it if allowed. (Board books are designed for this!) Since your baby will be just as interested in exploring what a book feels—and tastes—like as the story and pictures you are sharing, this list of special books your infant will enjoy keeps sturdiness in mind.

* *Look Look!* by Peter Linenthal (Dutton Juvenile, 1998) and other books in this series capitalize on the fact that young infants see black and white better than colors. Stunning, sharp images are sure to captivate most babies.

* *Monkey See, Monkey Zoo!* by Gerald Hawksley (Lamaze, Cloth Edition, 2001) is one of many books made entirely of fabric. Babies enjoy the softness and different fabric textures used in this book that follows a child's visit to the zoo.

* *Peek-a Who?* by Nina Laden (Chronicle, 2000) uses gentle rhymes and mysterious images behind die-cut holes to keep babies guessing at what's behind the next page.

* *Peekaboo Kisses* by Barney Saltzberg (Red Wagon Books, 2002) has everything babies love. There are large flaps to lift, a squeaky noise, different textures, and a mirror on the last page.

* *Smile!* by Roberta Grobel Intrater (Cartwheel, 1997) shows photographs of smiling babies. Since babies love to look at faces and enjoy looking at other babies, this one is sure to be a hit. To expose your child to different emotions, also explore books that show babies with different expressions.

* *Ten Little Ladybugs* by Melanie Gerth (Piggy Toes Press, 2007) is a pretty, sturdy book with plastic ladybugs that stick up from holes in the book's pages. Babies will have fun trying to touch the ladybugs as you read.

* *That's Not My Puppy . . .* by Fiona Watt (Usborne, 2001) "Its coat is too hairy." So states the mouse narrator as he looks at the puppy on the cover, going on to touch several different puppies—each with an interesting texture or color—until he finds his own puppy at the end of the book. Other books in this Touchy-Feely series give the same treatment to dinosaurs, trucks, trains, teddies, monkeys, and more.

Special Books for Your Toddler

Although some toddlers have little patience for books, many children love to be read to at this age. Bedtime is a good time for reading; children are more likely to be still when they are tired. You should try to introduce books you like since your toddler may insist on reading the same book over and over. Because toddlers are notoriously rough on books, be sure to supervise the reading of any books with paper pages. Below is a list of special books your toddler—and you—may enjoy.

* *Bark, George* by Jules Feiffer (HarperCollins, 1999) tells the story of George, a dog who cannot bark, even when his mother tells him to. He can make all kinds of other noises, though. A visit to the vet helps George and his mother get to the root of the problem.

* *The Going to Bed Book* by Sandra Boynton (Little Simon, 2004) is a standout among nighttime books because of its nautical theme. Boynton, who is also a songwriter, captures the silliness of a young child's bedtime, along with the rocking of the boat as a natural, relaxing background rhythm that soothes all of the characters to sleep.

* *The Little Mouse, the Red Ripe Strawberry, and the Big Hungry Bear* by Don Wood and Audrey Wood (Child's Play International, 1998) uses an unusual technique of having the narrator speak directly to a character—the mouse. This is a good book to reinforce sharing (something toddlers often find difficult) and introduce the concepts of whole and half.

* *No, David!* by David Shannon (Blue Sky Press, 1998) shows toddlers how they look when they are at their worst but also reminds them that their mommies love them anyway. Toddlers will enjoy asking what David is doing. Let them supply their own answers!

* *One Yellow Lion* by Matthew Van Fleet (Dial, 1992) introduces numbers, colors, and animals, all at once. The drawings are large, clear, and cute, and the foldout pictures of all of the animals interacting are a fun surprise that will inspire your child to recall and count which animal group matches each number.

* *School Bus* by Donald Crews (Greenwillow Books, 1993) is a must for children whose fancy is captured by these yellow giants. A free-form poem weaves together images of school buses making their morning and afternoon journeys through a town. The illustrations combine bright, vibrant forms and soft watercolor wash with a soothing text.

* *Teeth Are Not for Biting* by Elizabeth Verdick (Free Spirit Publishing, 2003) helps toddlers understand that biting other children hurts them and gives them better ideas about what to do with their teeth. This series includes companion books that teach children the negatives about hitting, name-calling, kicking, and even pulling animals' tails.

Special Books for Your Two-Year-Old

Two-year-olds are often ready to move beyond board books. As they develop a love for special books, they will want to choose what you read and often hold the books themselves. Supervise your child while reading books with paper pages because enthusiastic children will often tear them. Here are some books that will move your two-year-old from baby books to storybooks.

* *Fireman Small* by Wong Herbert Yee (Sagebrush, 2002) manages to combine a story about a fireman with soothing, skillful rhymes that will help your child wind down at the end of the day. This book is perfect for children who love fire trucks.

* *How Big Is a Pig?* by Claire Beaton (Barefoot Books, 2002) teaches about opposites using the actions and characteristics of animals. Rhyming text asks the title question on every page, and the unexpected answer at the end is quite funny.

* *I Love You as Much . . .* by Laura Krauss Melmed (HarperCollins, 2005) will make you remember how much you love your child even after a difficult day—which is why this book is recommended for children in the throes of the "terrible twos"! The illustrations show animals babies and mothers in their natural settings as the mothers tell the babies how much they love them.

* *The Monster at the End of This Book* by Jon Stone (Random House Books for Young Readers, 2000) is an old favorite. Grover (the Muppet) has heard that there is a monster at the end of the book, and he goes to great lengths to stop his reader from reaching the last page. After sarcasm, begging, and a brick wall don't stop the reader in her tracks, Grover happily realizes that the monster in the book isn't so scary after all.

* *Secret Seahorse* by Stella Blackstone (Barefoot Books, 2007) uses fabric collage art to help conceal a seahorse that hides on each page. It's an easy version of the many search-and-find books that are available.

* *Tails* by Matthew Van Fleet (Harcourt, 2003) takes touching textures and pulling flaps to the extreme while describing different kinds of animal tails. Although this is a rather delicate book with lots of paper pieces that might be pulled off, it's worth the extra caution to see a two-year-old scratch, sniff, and shout about the skunk's truly stinky tail; it never gets old.

Special Books for Your Three-Year-Old

Three-year-olds are ready for books with humor, and they are very interested in the world around them. They are also developing more empathy and learning how to play together instead of side by side. Use these choices to entertain and keep children engaged as their minds expand.

✳ *Animals Should Definitely Not Wear Clothing* by Judi Barrett (Aladdin, 1989) shows children that nothing is funnier than animals dressed up in 1970s clothing. From a giraffe wearing multiple neckties to a hen attempting to lay an egg while wearing pants, these animals demonstrate exactly why no clothing is necessary for our animal friends.

✳ *Baby Beluga* by Raffi (Crown Books for Young Readers, 1997) will be a favorite with younger ones because of the song, but three-year-olds will have many questions about this book, like *What is that house made of?* and *Why does that animal have a horn?* The gentle drawings of the animals from the Arctic Circle are as instructive as the song is fun to sing.

✳ *Charlie the Caterpillar* by Dom DeLuise (Aladdin, 1993) depicts a caterpillar who has a hard time making friends because they don't like the way he looks—until he becomes a beautiful butterfly, of course. This book effectively reinforces the lesson that it hurts to be excluded.

✳ *I Read Signs* by Tana Hoban (Greenwillow, 1987) uses bright, clear photographs to give children a closer look at the signs they see outside of the car window. This book will have your child looking for signs all over town—and possibly recognizing the words on some of them, as well.

✳ *Old Hat, New Hat* by Stan and Jan Berenstain (Random House Books for Young Readers, 1970) captures the feeling of what is great about old toys and comfy clothes. This book is excellent for teaching adjectives at a time when children's language is expanding to include more description. Repetitive language lends itself to fun and easy reading aloud.

✳ *The Pout-Pout Fish* by Deborah Diesen (Farrar, Straus and Giroux, 2008) tells the story of a fish who is pouty and sad until a smooch changes his outlook on life. The illustrations are very funny and engaging.

✳ *Sheep in a Jeep* by Nancy Shaw (Sandpiper, 2006) is a bouncing, rollicking tale of sheep who take a road trip and get into all kinds of mishaps.

✳ *Stranger in the Woods: A Photographic Fantasy* by Carl R. Sams II (C. R. Sams II Photography, 2000) is a story built around a series of amazing, clear photographs of animals that visit a snowman built just for them.

✳ *Time to Say "Please"!* by Mo Willem (Hyperion, 2005) helps to teach manners gently. The fun and somewhat complex illustrations for this book will capture children's imagination as they learn the best times to say *please, thank you,* and *I'm sorry.*

Special Books for Your Four-Year-Old

Some four-year-olds are ready to read, and many are at least ready to sit through some longer, more complex books. Here is a list of books that will keep four-year-olds entertained and that will also introduce them to other skills.

✳ *Cloudy with a Chance of Meatballs* by Judi Barrett (Atheneum, 1982) is not a book for the fainthearted. The residents of the sleepy town of Chewandswallow eat their food as it falls from the sky—until things get out of hand.

✳ *How Are You Peeling? Foods with Moods* by Saxton Freymann and Joost Elffers (Scholastic, 2004) combines simple text with humanlike vegetables to examine a whole range of emotions. Not every character in this book is happy, and this book challenges children to think about how they feel, what makes them feel that way, and also what they do about it.

✳ *How I Became a Pirate* by Melina Long (Harcourt, 2003) tells a salty tale of a young boy who is sure his parents won't mind if he becomes a pirate—as long as he makes it back home in time for soccer practice. Aargh!

✳ *How to Lose All Your Friends* by Nancy Carlson (Puffin, 1997). This effective book shows characters demonstrating all of the behaviors that will make losing friends easy. As you read this book, be sure to let your child suggest what the character should do instead in each situation.

✳ *Listen to the Wind* by Greg Mortenson and Susan L. Roth (Dial, 2009) is the picture book version of a true story. Mortenson, a nurse, got lost while trying to climb the mountain K2 but stumbled on a small Pakistani village. As they nursed him back to health, he realized that the village children did their lessons by writing with sticks in the dirt. Mortenson decided to repay them by building a school—the first of over 50 he helped build in the area.

✳ *My Little Sister Ate One Hare* by Bill Grossman (Crown Books for Young Readers, 1996) tells the story of a boy who watches his sister eat some strange snacks. This book teaches counting as it incorporates humor and the "yuck factor" children at this age seem to love.

✳ *Scranimals* by Jack Prelutsky (Greenwillow Books, 2006) uses poetry to describe such amazing animals as the "Bananaconda" and the "Radishark." Children will delight in the mixed-up creatures and enjoy these accessible, yet sophisticated, poems.

✳ *Scuffy the Tugboat and His Adventures Down the River* by Gertrude Crampton (Golden Books, 2001) was written half a century ago but still easily captures and holds children's interest. Scuffy is a tugboat who is "meant for greater things" than a little boy's bathtub. Young readers will delight in the journey that takes him all the way to the ocean—almost.

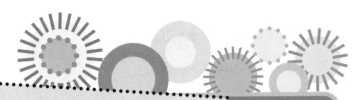

Special Books for Your Five-Year-Old

At five, your child seems much more like a "kid" than a baby. Most five-year-olds are getting ready to head off to kindergarten, which is a big deal for them and for their parents. Choose from this list of books to appeal to your child's growing mind and larger world.

❋ *First Day Jitters* by Julie Danneberg (Charlesbridge Publishing, 2000) captures the scary, jumpy feeling of going to school on the first day. Sarah has to be coaxed out of bed and into the car, finally joining a flood of children going into her new school. Students will be surprised when they find out Sarah is not who they think she is.

❋ *Have You Filled a Bucket Today? A Guide to Daily Happiness for Kids* by Carol McCloud (Nelson Publishing and Marketing, 2007) explains that filling an imaginary bucket with kind words is a great way to make others—and yourself—feel great. This book teaches that words are powerful.

❋ *The Kissing Hand* by Audrey Penn (Tanglewood Press, 2006) tells the tale of Chester Racoon who does not want to leave his mother to start school. She gives him a kiss on his hand and tells him how to use it to remind him of her all during his nights at school.

❋ *Miss Bindergarten Gets Ready for Kindergarten* by Joseph Slate (Puffin, 2001) follows a teacher and each of her students (with names from *A* to *Z*) as they get ready for the first day of school. Other books in this series mirror other important school events.

❋ *The Missing Piece* by Shel Silverstein (HarperCollins, 1976) contains a deceptively simple story and illustrations about what happens when you get what you thought you always wanted—but find out that it wasn't what you thought it would be.

❋ *Nate the Great* by Marjorie Weinman Sharmat (Delacorte Books for Young Readers, 2002) follows Nate the Great, amateur private eye, on one of his many amazing mystery cases. Simple text and short sentences tell a more complex story that is perfect for an emerging reader or curious five-year-old.

❋ *The One Hundredth Day of School!* by Abby Klein (Blue Sky Press, 2008) is a fun holiday to celebrate, and children are often asked to bring 100 of something to school. Freddy's classroom is no different—but how will Freddy ever get 100 shark trading cards in his collection when he only has 21?

❋ *Ramona the Pest* by Beverly Cleary (HarperCollins, 1992) will inspire giggles and sympathy as students listen to Ramona's exuberant adventures, including some trials and tribulations, during her exciting transition to kindergarten.

What to Do if Your Child Is Biting

As soon as children get teeth (and sometimes even before), they may start biting each other, their siblings, and even you. Ouch! Here are some reasons children bite and ideas for how to stop this painful habit.

❖ Babies and young toddlers often bite when they are teething. First, try to soothe your child's discomfort. Give her more attention and tell your child you understand that her mouth hurts—because it almost certainly does. Offer your child relief from her pain in the form of safe teething rings, a teething biscuit, or even a washcloth dipped in water, frozen, and thawing slightly. Monitor anything you give your child to chew, as always, and do not use anything that could be a choking hazard. Ask your child's pediatrician for suggestions if you think pain medication is needed.

❖ Toddlers bite for many reasons in addition to teething. They are learning to use their teeth and want to know what it feels like to bite into different things. A child sometimes confuses biting with kissing and gives a favorite classmate a nice, loving bite. Toddlers also bite out of aggression and frustration when someone takes a toy or otherwise disturbs their play. Biting is often a last resort when a child cannot win otherwise and wants to gain control of a situation. Your child may also bite when he realizes he gets attention for doing it, even if the attention is negative.

❖ The best way to deal with biting is to be proactive, intervening before the bite occurs and modeling alternative actions. If your child bites at home, watch for trigger behaviors that can tip you off before the bite happens. Some children have a biting "look" about them just before chomping down on a sibling. Others bite in certain situations, such as getting pushed or having a toy grabbed away by another child. Also, whenever possible, praise positive behavior rather than reacting to the biting behavior to give the biter more of the attention she craves.

❖ Try comforting the hurt child first. This will mean that the child who is biting does not get immediate attention, so the biting behavior is not reinforced.

❖ If you have a child who is biting at school or if your child has been bitten, be sure to talk to the school staff and work with them on changing this behavior!

Who is biting in here?

What to Do if Your Child Doesn't Want to Go to School

Most parents have carried a kicking, screaming, or crying child into school. It is not fun for you or your child. However, resisting being left at school is actually a normal developmental stage that most children pass through. Here are some ideas for making the transition easier for your child and for you!

❖ Prepare your child for where she is going. Bring your child to school to meet the teacher before the first day. If possible, arrange a playdate with a few of the children so that there are some familiar faces when she walks in.

❖ Make the beginning of the school year a happy event. A new lunch box, backpack, or outfit will brighten the day and make your child feel important, like he is *getting* to go to school rather than *having* to go to school.

❖ Don't make a big deal out of missing your child. If you tell her you will miss her so much, she will likely feel that she should miss you and be sad, too.

❖ As you walk into school, focus on your child. Do not talk on the phone or become too distracted chatting with other parents. Get down on his eye level to say good-bye and happily reassure him that you will be back soon.

❖ After you take your child safely to her classroom, say good-bye and leave promptly. Dragging out your good-bye only makes the separation worse. If your child is crying, it is for your benefit. She will probably stop very soon after you leave and she becomes interested in playing. The teachers will call you if she is inconsolable.

❖ It is often easier for a child to leave you than it is for him to be left by you. If your preschool has a drop-off service, try using it to see if it helps your child adjust to being separated more quickly.

❖ If your child does have a very hard time, stretch out her school day gradually. For example, have her stay only an hour for the first week, then an hour and a half the second week, and so on until she can comfortably stay for the full time.

❖ When you pick up your child, ask him open-ended questions about his day. If you ask him what he did and he says, "I painted," ask him about the colors he used, how big the paper was, what his friend painted, and whether or not his picture was dry before he left school.

❖ If your child needs reassurance, tell her how proud you are of her for staying at school. Remind her that you did indeed come back to get her.

❖ Tell your child a little about your day, as well. You are both getting important things done, and it is a good idea to compare notes.

❖ Finally, let your child help get herself ready for the next school day. Let her choose her outfit, pack her backpack, or help you make her lunch. These actions give her more control over some of the preparations for school and will allow her to feel like it is her decision to be happy about going.

Teaching Your Child to Be a Kind Friend

Knowing how to make friends and keep friendships is one of the most important life skills your child can have. All parents want their children to be kind and to have friends. Achieving the social and emotional maturity to do so is one of the main goals of most preschools. Use these ideas to help your child develop empathy, learn to play fair, and reach out to other children.

❖ You are your child's ultimate role model. Every kind word or action you do is sure to be noticed—and hopefully emulated—by your child, so take advantage of opportunities to show your child how you treat your friends.

❖ Create opportunities for your child to be a friend. Host playdates at your home. Give your child the chance to invite friends over; then, model for her how she should treat her guests.

❖ Some children need practice with recognizing social cues. Role-playing can help your child understand things like give-and-take in a conversation, appropriate volume, personal space, and eye contact. Practice playing "preschool" or "playdate" with your child. Encourage him to act like he does with his friends. Remind your child to look you in the eye when speaking. Gently guide him to stand an appropriate distance from you as you play, if necessary. Ask questions that show your interest in what he is doing if he needs help being comfortable responding to others. The more you practice with him, the less he will have to worry about whether he is acting like the other children.

❖ Shy children have a hard time expressing themselves to other children. If you notice your child does not converse easily with other children or seems unresponsive, ask her questions about what she wants to play. Getting a shy child past the awkwardness of initiating the play and into the play itself removes the barrier between your child and her friend and lets their common interest in the play take over.

❖ If your child initiates an argument or hits or bites another child, make sure he understands that he has hurt his friend. Help him to apologize sincerely and make amends by hugging his friend, giving back a toy he grabbed, etc.

❖ If your child and a friend are having a disagreement, try to elicit ideas from the two about how to solve the problem.

❖ When your child is the victim of another child's aggression, it can be a fine line between teaching her to stand up for herself and teaching her to retaliate. Hitting back is never a good idea. It does not teach children how to get beyond the hitting and usually escalates fighting. Encourage your child to use her words to make it clear how she feels. For example, teach her to say, "I was not finished with that toy. Please give it back. I will let you play with it when I am finished." Encourage your child to speak loudly if she wants to alert the teacher to the fact that she is having trouble with another child.

❖ When your child has used his words and the other child has not responded or continues to be aggressive, your child should let the teacher know what is going on. This does not mean telling the teacher things like, "I want that toy. Make him give it to me." But if he is hurt or does not know what to do next, a teacher should be able to intervene.

Bullying

Bullying is behavior by a child or group of children that causes mental distress and even physical harm to other children. Believe it or not, bullying starts in preschool. It isn't the kind of bullying you think of in, say, middle school—children don't take each other's lunch money or stuff each other into lockers. Instead, they say things like, "You are not my friend," or "You can't play with us." They do not have to use words, either. One child may single out another and continually knock down that child's block tower or take the child's toys away. Children who are smaller or younger than their classmates are often targets in toddler classrooms, while children who are exceptionally quiet and shy or who seem unlikely to stand up for themselves are often singled out in older classrooms. Children with disabilities or who act significantly different from their classmates can also be targets. They may not be picked on, but they are likely to be excluded. It is very important to address this behavior with preschoolers because children at this age are in the process of developing their social behaviors and their self-esteems. Behaviors they establish at this age can continue for a lifetime.

If your child is being bullied, he may ask to stay home from school, pretend to be sick, or specifically complain about another child and say he doesn't like someone in his class. There are several ways to help your child avoid becoming a target of bullying. As soon as your child can speak, help him understand that saying things like, "No!" "Please stop!" I don't like that!" and other phrases that tell how he feels will show other children that he is ready to stand up for himself. Encourage your child to use a firm voice that is loud enough for other children and the teacher to hear. If a teacher hears this kind of talk, she will pay attention to the situation before it gets out of hand. Also, make sure your child knows that if another child hurts him or destroys something he is making, he should tell the teacher after he uses his words.

If your child is being a bully, you may not be aware of it. If she complains that other children exclude her, try to find out why. Ask specific questions about what she does while playing with others. Talk to your child's teacher about her relationships. Also, try inviting several of your child's friends over and watch the children's interactions. If your child excludes one child, is rougher or more aggressive than all of the other children, cannot keep her hands to herself, or is unfriendly in her words or actions, or if the other children seem especially timid around her, she may be bullying others and causing other children to avoid her. You will need to work with your child to show her how to be a kind friend to others. Role-play preschool with your child and model alternatives to behavior that causes her to lose friends.

If you suspect your child is bullying others at school or is being bullied, it's time to have a talk with the teacher. Arrange for a conference, ask how your child interacts with others at school, and be open to what she has to say. She will probably have some good suggestions on how to work with your child at home if he is having trouble making and keeping friends or if he is being mistreated by other children.

Stranger Danger

If your child is not immediately comfortable at preschool with new classroom teachers, pat yourself on the back. A child should not be instantly at ease with strangers. Stranger anxiety is common among preschoolers, and it is a healthy reaction to an unfamiliar situation that could possibly be dangerous.

❖ By the age of two, parents should talk to their children about strangers. It is hard to explain why it is fine to wave at a friendly person at the grocery store, while it is not okay to get in that person's car. It is also hard to encourage independence in almost every situation, but to discourage it when your child runs out of your sight at the mall or won't hold your hand in a crowd of people or a parking lot.

❖ Although we all try our best, it is impossible to have your eye on your child at every minute. Explain to your child that if she does not know someone very well, she should never go anywhere with that person. Tell your child that no matter what the stranger says, she should never go with or take anything from someone unless you say it is okay. Strangers may offer candy, ask a child for help to look for a lost puppy, tell a child that her parents have asked the stranger to pick her up at school, or just ask the child for a hug. Make sure your child knows that NONE of these things are safe. When your child is approached by a stranger, she should yell and run away to find you unless you are there to control the situation.

❖ Also, make your child aware that some places are less safe than others. Public restrooms, parking lots, parks, busy sidewalks, busy roads, public playgrounds, sporting events, or any place where there is a large crowd can be a dangerous place. Do not tell your child he should not go where you cannot see him. Instead, tell him he should not go where *he* cannot see *you*. Young children always assume their parents are watching, and they can easily wander off for this reason. Practice having your child respond immediately by answering you and walking to your side when you call him.

❖ Finally, if you allow your child to use a computer at all, make sure she is constantly supervised and do not allow her to chat online unless it is with a close friend or family member. Many predators use the Internet to reach children. Even if they cannot have physical contact with your child, they can still do a lot of damage with inappropriate words or pictures.

❖ This is not a pleasant topic for you or your child. It can be frightening and also distressing if a child feels he overreacted or used the wrong behavior. It can also be hard to explain why one minute you encourage your child to say hi to the nice lady who waved and the next minute tell him not to talk to strangers. Make sure your child knows that any time he is uncomfortable for any reason, he should find you immediately and not feel upset for not being nice to someone he does not know.

The Importance Of Eating Healthful Foods

Getting healthful food into a picky toddler or preschooler is a challenge. When infants begin eating baby food and solids, you can control their options, but as soon as they know there are other tastes and flavors, children begin to make their preferences known—sometimes loudly! Children must eat well in order to continue the incredible amount of brain and body growth they need to achieve—their bodies are doubling in size during their early years! To keep your child on track and encourage good eating habits that will last a lifetime, try some of these suggestions.

❖ Really think about what you offer to your child before serving it. Is this a food item that will help with growth and give your child enough energy to last until the next scheduled meal or snack time? Or, is it only going to provide a sugar rush and cause your child to crash and be cranky later?

❖ Offer healthy options whenever possible. When healthful foods are all that there is to eat, often, children will eat them.

❖ If your child refuses a new food, try again—and again. Expect this to be a long process, but take heart—remember all of the foods you used to think were yucky?

❖ Make it fun. Cut food into shapes with cookie cutters. Spear fruit with craft sticks to make kabobs. Make "gorp" by mixing treats and healthful snacks together.

❖ Add healthful ingredients to foods your child will eat. Mix cooked and mashed carrots or squash into macaroni and cheese or add pureed cauliflower to mashed potatoes.

❖ Monitor your child's eating. Do not let your child eat a whole bag of salty crackers just because it's more convenient for you. Instead, offer a few crackers along with cheese cubes and some slices of apple or orange.

❖ Limit fast food. Despite the convenience, the drive-through is not a great option for a toddler or preschooler. If you must eat fast food, choose some of the more healthful options now available.

❖ Let your children help you garden and cook. They are often more likely to eat food they have grown and prepared themselves.

❖ Serve the foods you most want your child to eat first. If you put all of the food on the plate at the same time, children will usually go for the macaroni and cheese and claim to be full when it's time to eat the green stuff.

❖ Eat healthful foods yourself. Children imitate their parents. If they see you grab a sausage biscuit, they are less likely to find a yogurt-and-fruit parfait appealing.

❖ Serve children the same foods you eat to expand their palates. If you make yourself a chicken taco salad with lettuce and tomatoes, it's fine to "deconstruct" the salad, offering the meat, lettuce, tomatoes, and other elements separately since many children do not like to mix foods.

Keeping Your Child Active

Preschoolers always seem to have more than their fair share of energy to expel. This can become a problem since sometimes preschoolers' energy is not expressed in the most positive way. But, they have to get rid of that excess energy somehow, and they need guidance to know how to express themselves appropriately through movement. Keeping children active at a young age increases the possibility that they will stay active for years to come. Here are some ways to help your preschooler be active in more ways than one and hopefully give you a little break at the same time.

❖ Go outside. It's the simplest solution, even on days when the weather is not great. Fresh air and a change of scenery help children release pent-up energy. Grab the all-weather gear in rain or snow. Puddles and drifts are great for adding extra movement!

❖ Get involved in a game. You can play cards or board games as well as outside sports. Children do not have to use their bodies for all active participation; their brains can be involved in play as well. Learning how to take turns, knowing the rules of the game, and practicing good sportsmanship all involve active participation.

❖ Provide creative art tools on a table—cover it with newspaper if you are worried about the mess. Painting, kneading play dough, cutting with scissors, gluing, and using stickers will all help keep preschoolers' creative juices flowing. Let them express themselves freely and try not to direct them too much. Be sure to display their masterpieces when their work is finished. Even if it looks like scribbles to you, it is important work that deserves praise.

❖ Give your child a chance to try using tools. Letting your child hammer golf tees into plastic foam is a great way to help her release tension and use her muscles. Or, offer a measuring tape and help her measure herself, the table, the door, etc. This activity can evolve into more elaborate work if you wish to bring out hammers, nails, and wood, but using simple materials works just as well.

❖ Don't wait for bath time—fill the bathtub and let your child get in! Place towels on the floor to absorb excess water and let your child be free in the tub. Offer measuring cups, sifters, washcloths, plastic dolls, plastic blocks, and even goggles. Let your child explore how water moves, how it cleans, water safety, and more. This can fill up an entire afternoon with fun.

❖ Turn on your favorite music and have a dance party. If you find children's music less than entertaining, substitute your own favorites. (Make sure beforehand that any songs you choose contain only lyrics you won't mind hearing your child sing later!) Add a paper towel tube for a microphone, a tennis racket guitar, and pots and pans for the drum section and help your child create the rock band you always wanted.

Potty Time!

If your child is between the ages of two and four, you are in prime time for potty training. This can be one of the most challenging things you teach your young child—probably because you want your child to learn SO BADLY and to be done with diapers. Here are some tips for potty training and making the transition from home to school.

❖ Don't rush your child into potty training or push him to start before he is ready. This and eating are the two things over which your child has absolute control. Trying to take away that control will frustrate you and make your child resist—because he can.

❖ Children all develop at different rates and are physically ready at different times. One two-year-old may have great bladder control and awareness, while another may not. Follow your child's cues to be able to tell when she is ready. For example, if her diaper remains dry overnight or during nap time, if she talks about using the potty and shows great interest, and if she starts telling you she needs to go, then she may be ready to start potty training.

❖ Before you expect your child to use a potty, prepare him for the mechanics of it. Make sure you have a potty your child can easily reach and help him learn to pull down his own pants, unroll toilet paper, practice wiping, and pull up his pants again. These tasks are hard skills for small children to acquire.

❖ There are as many ways to potty train a child as there are children. Each child will respond differently to different methods. Rewards (stickers, candy treats, cool new underwear, etc.) will work for some children. Bribing is definitely okay when potty training a child. However, be consistent when handing out rewards. Choose a small reward to give each time or use stickers on an incentive chart and work toward a goal.

❖ Other children (especially boys) respond to targets in the potty. Float a few cereal pieces in the toilet and let your child have "target practice." This also helps your child pay attention and not sprinkle the floor.

❖ Some children just need time. Provide a basket of small toys and books near the potty to encourage your child to linger. Some parents even allow toilet sitting while playing a handheld game or watching television. This works especially well to calm a child who is anxious about staying there or to encourage a child who just wants to get up and move around.

❖ Do not ask your child if she has to go. Most children will say that they don't. Instead, regularly make your child sit on the potty. If necessary, set a timer every 30 minutes to remind both of you of the schedule.

❖ Once your child is in underwear, try not to revert to pull-on training pants—be consistent. Expect accidents and carry a few changes of clothing with you at all times. If your child wets his pants, don't get upset. He will get it eventually.

❖ Finally, whatever method you use, be consistent and patient and make it fun! Your child is learning something new, and, just like any other new thing, it takes time to master. Just remember, your child will not go to middle school in diapers!